BRIGHT NOTES

NOTES FROM THE UNDERGROUND BY FYODOR DOSTOYEVSKY

Intelligent Education

Nashville, Tennessee

BRIGHT NOTES: Notes From the Underground
www.BrightNotes.com

No part of this publication may be used or reproduced in any manner whatsoever without written permission, except in the case of brief quotations in critical articles and reviews. For permissions, contact Influence Publishers http://www.influencepublishers.com.

ISBN: 978-1-645421-38-2 (Paperback)
ISBN: 978-1-645421-39-9 (eBook)

Published in accordance with the U.S. Copyright Office Orphan Works and Mass Digitization report of the register of copyrights, June 2015.

Originally published by Monarch Press.
Leslie A. Juhasz, 1965
2020 Edition published by Influence Publishers.

Interior design by Lapiz Digital Services. Cover Design by Thinkpen Designs.

Printed in the United States of America.

Library of Congress Cataloging-in-Publication Data forthcoming.
Names: Intelligent Education
Title: BRIGHT NOTES: Notes From the Underground
Subject: STU004000 STUDY AIDS / Book Notes

CONTENTS

1)	Introduction to Fyodor Dostoyevsky	1
2)	Textual Analysis	
	Part 1: Underground	8
	Part 2: Apropos of The Wet Snow	22
3)	Character Analyses	55
4)	Critical Commentary	60
5)	Essay Questions and Answers	68
6)	Bibliography	77

INTRODUCTION TO FYODOR DOSTOYEVSKY

BIOGRAPHICAL SKETCH OF DOSTOYEVSKY

Fyodor Mikhailovich Dostoyevsky was born October 30, 1821 in Moscow, the second son of Mikhail, a physician at the Maryinski Hospital for the Poor. The family belonged to the hereditary nobility and possessed a small country estate worked by some one hundred "souls" as serfs were then called. Late every spring the family left Moscow to spend the summer there.

After Fyodor completed his secondary education, his father sent him in 1838 to St. Petersburg where he entered the College of Engineers, a military school run by the Czar. Although he studied hard and in general made a good impression on his teachers, the young cadet was in constant financial straits. Always writing home for more money, he describes his "terrible plight" in the most urgent terms. When money came, though, he celebrated its arrival with a huge banquet and drinking party for his friends, or gambled it away shooting pool. He was generous to the point of self-destruction. When his brother Mikhail was married, Fyodor sent him one hundred fifty rubles. Two weeks later he was broke again, begging him for five. This inability to manage his finances persisted throughout his life. In fact, he was nearly always on the brink of bankruptcy.

Despite his ups and downs in Petersburg, the twenty-three-year-old Dostoyevsky became so attached to the city that the mere thought of living elsewhere was unbearable for him. So when he learned that he was about to be posted to the provinces, he resigned his commission and resolved to support himself by writing. In 1846 *Poor Folk* was published and immediately became a best seller. The young author was lionized as the new Gogol, received into the best houses, and became the object of unrestrained praise. The novel is a brilliantly written though sentimental story about the destructive effects of poverty. In quick succession there followed *The Double* (1846) and a collection of short stories under the title *White Nights* (1848).

About this time Dostoyevsky became seriously ill, both mentally and physically. Poor, quarrelsome, the victim of unpredictable fevers and convulsions, he soon alienated his admirers as well as his editors. Furthermore, since his erratic behavior was put down to personality rather than to the illness that it was, he was frequently laughed at, jeered, and mocked. Turgenev, for instance, so despised him that he would engage him in conversation merely for the pleasure of torturing him. Still, Dostoyevsky was reckoned among the most promising young writers of the day. Unfortunately, his literary career was suddenly interrupted by a remarkable incident that was the direct consequence of his political involvement.

SENTENCED TO DEATH

Ever since the Decembrist revolt in 1825 it had become fashionable for men of learning to promote social reform. Revolutionary manifestoes were printed abroad, smuggled into the country, and widely distributed. Czar Nicholas I, however, was determined that there would be no revolution in Russia under him. Censorship was severe and many domestic and foreign authors were banned. The penalties for revolutionary activity were increased, and government spies were everywhere. Notwithstanding, Dostoyevsky joint a group of political rebels who met every Friday evening at Mikhail Petrashevsky's apartment. Here they discussed different political trends, plotting revolution on the side in a rather harmless way. All the same, the government became suspicious. The members of the circle were arrested, brought to trial, and Dostoyevsky, along with several others, was sentenced to death.

Finally, on a cold winter morning after a miserable stay in prison, the future author and his co-conspirators were driven to their place of execution. There, tied to stakes, the unlucky men faced the firing squad. However, as the soldiers were given the order to aim, a horseman suddenly appeared riding full tilt across the square. He bore a letter from the Czar commuting all the death sentences to prison terms. The entire affair was prearranged to frighten them and others of their kind into submission to the Czarist regime.

"TO LIVE, NO MATTER HOW"

Needless to say, Dostoyevsky was profoundly affected by this brief encounter with death. So much so in fact that the theme of the condemned man appears on countless occasions in his letters, articles, and novels. Among the most forceful passages describing the condemned man's state of mind occurs in *Crime and Punishment* when Raskolnikov says: "Someone condemned to death thinks an hour before his death that if he had to live on a steep pinnacle or on a rock or on a cliff edge so narrow that there was only room to stand, and around him there were abysses, the ocean, and everlasting darkness, eternal solitude, eternal tempests - if he had to remain standing on a few square inches of space for a thousand years or all eternity, it would be better to live than to die. Only to live, to live, to live, no matter how."

Dostoyevsky's will to live was severely tested by the Czar's verdict. He was sentenced to four years' hard labor in Siberia followed by another five as a common soldier in a penal battalion. The years of physical hardship, loneliness, and the study of the Bible, the only reading allowed the prisoners, completely changed the author's way of thinking. In both religion and politics he turns into an outspoken conservative, a staunch supporter of the Czarist regime, and the Russian Orthodox Church. He becomes convinced that an Orthodox Christian will, of his own accord, subject himself joyfully to the will of God. Furthermore, by some mystic fiat, a true Russian's political strivings will miraculously coincide with the will of the Czar Emancipator. These attitudes form the basis of Dostoyevsky's dialectical thought and ultimately determine whether his heroes are saved or destroyed.

Thus when in 1859, ten years after his arrest, Dostoyevsky is permitted to resign from the army and return to Petersburg, we meet a changed writer, but not a less productive one. Shortly after his release he publishes an account of his imprisonment, *Notes from the House of the Dead* (1860). This is followed by the short novel *The Insulted and the Injured* (1861). He even tries his hand at journalism, successfully editing his own paper. Unfortunately, his troubles with the regime are not over. His journal, *Vremya*, is considered subversive and ordered closed. Disgusted, Dostoyevsky decides to leave Russia for Europe.

In Wiesbaden he won a large sum of money which allowed him the luxury of an affair with the beautiful, charming, and intelligent Polina Suslova. They toured Europe together visiting all the "in" places until he lost his money. Possessing a destructive passion for gambling, he could not keep away from the casinos. On several occasions he lost everything and had to write friends in Russia for the fare home.

The novel *The Gambler* (1866) is a thinly veiled autobiographical account of this trip. The book is also the third major work in the most productive period of his life which begins in 1864 with the publication of *Notes from Underground*. During the next sixteen years Dostoyevsky worked feverishly, producing among other things five major novels and *The Diary of a Writer*. In addition, he maintained a voluminous correspondence with friends, acquaintances, and various admirers who wrote for advice.

MARRIAGE AND FAME

Dostoyevsky's existence changed for the better with his marriage to Anna Snitkina, his secretary. Among her many qualities was a good business sense that enabled her to offset her husband's inability to manage his finances. There were trips abroad and every summer the family rented a small cottage in the country. Dostoyevsky could now truly enjoy his fame as one of Russia's leading authors and was finally able to write at his leisure.

Yet Dostoyevsky's health was always bad. Since his return from Siberia he suffered from epilepsy and these attacks increased with alarming frequency in the 1860s. During the worst period the fits came once a month and so exhausted him that he needed several days to recover. In addition, he contracted tuberculosis in the 1870s which, together with lung cancer, precipitated his death January 28, 1881.

ST. PETERSBURG: DOSTOYEVSKY'S BAD DREAM

The background of many of the author's stories, Dostoyevsky's St. Petersburg seems to be a flat, featureless wasteland. Its buildings lack character and its streets are dismal alleyways rarely touched by daylight. To Dostoyevsky, St. Petersburg seemed often so unreal that he was haunted by the prospect that it was simply someone's dream and that upon awakening everything would disappear leaving only the marshes and lakes. Others had felt likewise before him. When Peter the Great realized his ambition to build a city upon the Finnish marsh, the peasants living in the vicinity thought that it had been pulled down from the sky. It is only fitting that in such a city human activity is subdued. There is no hustle and bustle in Dostoyevsky's city streets, nor do we find the comforting noise of people going about their daily business. Rarely anything takes place in open daylight. The city seems to be condemned to perpetual twilight through which Dostoyevsky's characters hurry to their non-descript lodgings.

Thus, Dostoyevsky never describes a city in the manner of Balzac. In fact, he had an antipathy toward any kind of description of buildings or landscapes, saying that he had better things to do than waste time over creating word pictures. Consequently, he draws the barest outlines and leaves the reader to fill in the details. From another angle, this method is all the more effective because it allows the reader to create his own image of the city.

We could say that the author conceives St. Petersburg like a map. He chooses a location and then strictly adheres to its dimensions. In *Crime and Punishment*, for example, we know exactly where Raskolnikov lives, how many paces to the moneylender's house, and how far it is to the police station. Often Dostoyevsky's favorite places are the ones he personally knows. Central to *Crime and Punishment* is Haymarket Square close to which the author lived for many years. An unbelievably filthy quarter, it is the gathering place of thieves, prostitutes and the like. Surrounding the square are the stalls from which are hawked all manner of merchandise of use only to the destitute. Leading off the square are trash-filled alleyways bordered by pothouses and bodakings of the worst kind. Like Raskolnikov, Dostoyevsky loved to wander aimlessly about the place filling his lungs with the fetid air as if he were inhaling the essence of being. Still, precise descriptions of the place are absent. The scenery resembles a rather hastily erected stage set. Yet, we sense it as real because the characters are real, often uncomfortably so.

NOTES FROM THE UNDERGROUND

TEXTUAL ANALYSIS

PART 1: UNDERGROUND

In a footnote to the title the author remarks that though the diary is fictional, the person described therein "must exist" given the conditions of contemporary society.

Comment

This prefacing remark is significant because it shows that Dostoyevsky did not regard the case of the underground man as a curious anomaly whose interest lies in its rarity. He thought of the "underground" as representative of the state in which many persons must live in modern society. This condition is not typical of the Russian masses, but it is similar to the lot of many among the intelligentsia. In fact, he later asserted in his notebook that the chief merit of the *Notes* was that it laid bare the reality of this particular Russian type, exposing "its disfigured and tragic side."

The narrator introduces himself as a sick, unattractive, and spiteful man. He knows he should consult a physician about his illness, a liver ailment, but he refuses to do so out of spite. He knows this is illogical: he is punishing himself instead of the doctors; yet he will not seek medical aid.

Comment

At the very beginning, Dostoyevsky wishes to illustrate the contradictions inherent in the self. The Classicists usually described types as characters consumed by one desire, often one obsessive consideration. The Romantics were the first to suggest the width of the scale of emotions possessed by a person. Realism, the next literary school, accepted the fact of man's complexity but tried to explain it in scientific terms. Dostoyevsky's aim is to prove that man's character does not lend itself to scientific scrutiny. We shall analyze this later in greater detail.

He is now forty years old. He used to be a civil servant. He was always grumpy and contemptuous of those asking for information, even though most of these were poor, timid people. There was an officer, however, who would not be humbled, but kept clanking his sword.

Comment

The underground man's age coincides with Dostoyevsky's. Moreover, they both were at one time in the civil service and left it on their own.

But the worst thing about it all was that, though he always acted spiteful, actually he was not an angry, not even an embittered man! He was lying when he said at the start that he was a spiteful official. He was lying out of spite. In actuality, he was conscious of many stirrings in himself diametrically opposed to anger while he was acting spiteful. But he was ashamed to admit to anything else than rancor.

Comment

So far, we have seen that he was more than merely an embittered person - he had, simultaneously, other emotions which for some reason he would not acknowledge. This would mean that his self is wider, more complicated, and can even simultaneously contain contradictory elements. In other terms, the person is richer and more complex than one usually admits.

Was his problem then, he asks, that he could not make himself angry? No, it was more serious. He could not become anything, neither mad nor kind, neither a hero nor an insect.

Comment

Thus, beyond the fact that the person exists on a wider scope than we imagine or pretend, he confronts a more basic difficulty, that of not being genuinely anything. Unlike the protagonist of Franz Kafka's famous *Metamorphosis,* he does not have the consolation of being able to define himself as a cockroach: he cannot even say he is an insect.

What is the narrator's lamentable condition due to? The reason is this: an intelligent man cannot become anything in earnest; a nineteenth-century intellectual is condemned to be a characterless creature.

Comment

Here we have the key to his predicament: it is intelligence. But why does he claim that intelligence prevents us from defining ourselves? Should we not know ourselves better if we have been provided with more brains? We shall learn the answer soon.

For the sole purpose of having enough money to eat, the underground man joined the service. He was a collegiate assessor. But last year he inherited 6,000 rubles and he immediately quit. He is living in a squalid room in the suburbs. His servant is an old peasant woman, smelly and ill-natured. The climate of the city is not good for him; moreover, he knows full well that he could live much cheaper elsewhere; yet he will not move. Why? Well, what difference does it all make?

Comment

The locale of the story is Saint Petersburg (Leningrad), capital of Russia from 1712 until 1917. Peter the Great, who founded it, built it over reclaimed marshes. Hence the allusion to the unhealthful climate.

The underground man has many a time tried to become an insect. But he was not up to it; he is too conscious. A higher level of consciousness is an illness. A cultivated man of the nineteenth century has about four times more of it than he needs. But none are worse off than the unlucky inhabitants of Petersburg, most imaginary and theoretical of all towns on the globe. Men of action, direct persons, are the only ones who have the right dosage of consciousness.

Comment

It becomes clear now that intelligence is understood by Dostoyevsky as consciousness. The notion that consciousness is a curse originates in modern literature with the German Romantics, particularly with E.T.A. Hoffmann, whose works were well known by the author. Let us have a closer look at the import of Dostoyevsky's words, for here we are faced with the crux of the problem exposed in the book, as well as one of the main themes of contemporary philosophy and literature. The malady of the underground man is actually self-consciousness: he is endowed with the faculty of introspection. An animal presumably responds to stimuli with instinctive emotive reactions: fear, anger, joy, etc. A completely "natural" man would be like an animal; he would never question himself. Self-consciousness makes us look at ourselves as if in a mirror. Under the searchlight of reflexive consciousness, the emotions evaporate, and the more we try to establish the data we seek, the less we are likely to see. The moment the spiteful official wanted to make sure he was a spiteful official, spite itself disappeared, and he was merely playing a role, and a false one at that. This interesting phenomenon of the emptying of consciousness as soon as it is directed inward led Auguste Comte, the French positivist philosopher, to the conclusion that introspection was impossible. The same considerations lie at the basis of Jean-Paul Sartre's existentialism. The man whom Dostoyevsky calls direct or the "man of action" acts on impulse and instinct alone and consequently never has to face the torments experienced by the narrator.

To say that one is ill constitutes a fashionable affectation in our times - yet, he affirms, consciousness is a real disease. But to leave that subject for a minute, he continues, why is it that at the most solemn and subtle moments in life, when one should be permeated with serene or lofty sentiments, invariably the ugliest and most grotesque thoughts occur to him? Actually, he has not only thought but done the most despicable things just when he knew he should have acted nobly.

Comment

The antithesis he refers to is what the later Romantics called irony. They could no longer deny the absurdities inherent in the conception of the romantic hero. Romanticism represents a step toward freedom as opposed to Classicism, yet it painstakingly avoids any mention of certain aspects of reality. The last Romantics could not yet break with the former ideals, but already indicated a dualism such as Dostoyevsky outlines here, an oscillation between the sublime and the ridiculous, the lofty and depraved. The underground man himself is influenced by the romantic ideals of his upbringing, while he cannot fail to notice that reality is more complex.

He was ashamed of this contradiction, because he thought it was different with other people. He got to such a point of depravity that his very tortured condition, the thought of having done something despicable and loathsome used to turn into a kind of sweetness, a positive enjoyment. He used to sit at night alone in a corner, in his despised living quarters, thinking that he had reached the last rung, that there was nowhere to go, that everything had been definitively and irretrievably lost - and get a morbid enjoyment out of it.

Comment

Here and elsewhere one cannot deny the existence of certain masochistic tendencies in the narrator. He derives pleasure from punishing himself. In the case of the underground man, masochism appears indeed as a perversion, the turning of aggression against the subject itself.

Yes, he insists, there have been times when he would have been happy had someone beaten him to a pulp. It is useless to deny that everything that has happened to him has been through his own fault, though strictly speaking he cannot blame even himself, for what has acted in him was simply a law of nature. He is sure that if someone attacked him he would not try to revenge himself. Whereas, what happens to a direct, natural person when he has taken offense? His entire being is possessed with the idea of revenge, so that there remains nothing else left in it. On the other hand, the man of acute consciousness will be so bedeviled by questions and doubts that he will turn everything inside out until there will be no conviction left in his mind of the justice of his planned revenge.

Comment

Aside from his problem of introspection, the underground man cannot act because he sees both sides of every question. He is rendered inactive by the fact that, as we pointed out above, he cannot identify completely with any emotion, but this is also connected with another aspect of his intellectuality: he sees extramental reality in its complexity.

All the overconscious man can do is creep ignominiously into his hole like a mouse. And there he will re-enact for himself the whole humiliating scene, never forgetting a detail, wallowing in shame, nursing his spite, until his death comes.

Comment

Unfortunately, Dostoyevsky does not merely point out the contradictions in the self but he is at times guilty of contradicting himself. Before, he argued that the underground man could not become anything; now we see that he can have an authentic experience of spite and shame; later on there will be other emotional states mentioned without any question of identification. The answer to this contradiction is that his mental affliction is not quite so radical as he first stated: he does of course experience emotions, but he cannot find complete identification with these. This is the state that Sartre will later call the ever-present question in one's consciousness of the authenticity of one's existence.

The underground man can even find a kind of perverse enjoyment in a toothache. When he has a toothache, he moans; but this is not a natural reaction as it would be with a peasant. No, his moans are designed to let everyone know that he is suffering. He savors the feeling of his degradation. Why does he go through all these capers? Fundamentally, out of sheer boredom: one has to do something with oneself. Just to amuse himself, he has often pretended to be offended, and played the game so well that in the end he really felt offended. At other times he tried to convince himself that he was in love. He was jealous, beside himself, while all the while he knew it was mockery; it was all from ennui.

Comment

The considerations given in the paragraph above suggest a theory of the emotions akin to that developed by the existentialists in our own century. They claim that emotions are not spontaneous responses, not "physiological storms" as propounded by traditional psychology, but attitudes consciously chosen by the subject. For the time being, it would seem, though, that the underground man has found one true underlying motive: boredom.

What joy he would have experienced, had he been able to say truthfully that boredom or sluggishness lay at the bottom of all his actions! He would have respected himself because he would have been at last defined as something - a lazy man. Being a sluggard is a vocation, a career. How perfect it all would have been! He used to know a gentleman who prided himself on being an expert on the life of Lafitte. He considered this to be his distinguishing mark, his identifying badge, and died with a tranquil conscience because of that conviction. Knowing that he was a sluggard and a glutton, the underground man would have flourished, would have colored a ruby nose for himself, would have been regarded as something real and solid by everyone.

Comment: The narrator constantly shifts his ground. As the book is supposedly the diary of a tormented soul and not a scientific disquisition this is not necessarily a fault, but the reader should be aware of these shifts. The context here is still the impossibility of identification, but because of the liquid quality of consciousness rather than because of introspection. Man exists primarily as a thinking process. This was the discovery of the idealists, of Berkeley (1685-1783) and his disciples. The German idealist philosopher Hegel (1770-1831) already called man a for-itself, and contemporary existentialist doctrine is largely based on this term. The underground man (and presumably Dostoyevsky) believes that others, the ones he calls natural or direct men, do not encounter the same difficulties in defining themselves as he does. According to the Sartreans this is due to the fact that we see others as objects, as solid bodies, whereas to ourselves we are subjects, a mere thinking process. One knows oneself as for-itself, whereas other people seem to be in-themselves. This is the underground man's mistake in supposing that the expert on Lafitte led a contented life.

Many modern thinkers subscribe to the proposition that man in the past has committed evil deeds only because he did not understand his own enlightened self-interest. They say that as soon as modern science can explain to man that crime and bloodshed are against his own interest, all evil will be eliminated and people will lead normal and happy lives ever after.

Comment

The philosophy he refers to is Jeremy Bentham's (1748-1832) utilitarianism. Dostoyevsky rebelled against the affirmation of the pleasure principle contained in Bentham's doctrine. Much of the argumentation that follows is an attempt to discredit it.

They think that they will be able then to predict all human actions, tabulate them according to the laws of nature, mathematically, like logarithms. There will be no incidents and chance occurrences left in the world. But these erudite gentlemen ignore one important feature about the human mind: that there is something dearer to it than its material self-interest. One may choose what is the opposite of one's advantage, simply for the sake of asserting one's freedom.

Comment

The gist of this is that utilitarianism will not work as a practical philosophy because man does not follow his narrowly interpreted self-interest, but may do things purely out of a desire to prove that he is free.

But, these gentlemen will object, the freedom of the will is but an **allusion** - what you imagine to be your free choice can be reduced by modern science to a mathematical formula. However, the underground man answers, man does not act according to reason. The whole of human life includes reason and the impulses. Even in the lives of the most moral and rational persons odd things keep turning up, they are continually being false to their cherished reason, and sometimes in the most unseemly ways.

Comment

The narrator (whose opinion on this issue coincides with Dostoyevsky's) repeats himself several times in the original, trying to prove that there is such a thing as a free action, but he seems to end up in a circle. To postulate the freedom of the will would appear to be an appeal to the irrational, but the irrational by definition cannot be proved by logical (i.e., rational) argument. A free act would be unmotivated. Even if just to prove the point that freedom exists I were to commit a totally senseless act, I would still have a motive, namely, the motive to prove that I have no motive. Logic demands that there should be a sufficient cause for every effect. Contradicting this is the direct experience of freedom that all of us have whenever we are forced to make a decision. Philosophers have been intrigued by this enigma throughout the ages. Dostoyevsky, who loathed the scientific determinism of the mid-nineteenth century, passionately wanted to demonstrate that man is not predictable. He thereby became the forerunner of a whole new school of thought that was to reject determinism and rationalism.

The law of logic is not the law of humanity. Mathematical certainty is fine, but it is not what man really needs. If we do away with all the mysteries, there will be nothing else to look for. Man loves the process of attaining, but can do nothing with its result. Two times two makes four is excellent logic, but two times two is five has a lot more charm to it. Man does not only want pleasure. He likes to suffer at times too. He will never renounce suffering, for he yearns for destruction and chaos.

Comment

Dostoyevsky's argument is becoming less and less effective here, as he goes off on several unrelated tangents. First, to say that man does not like the notion of being found predictable is not to disprove determinism. Secondly, he fails to distinguish between internal and external reality. That we must always set new goals for ourselves, never being satisfied with what we have, may very well be true, yet it has nothing to do with free will. Finally, the assertion that people often choose to suffer rather than to be happy is a play on words. In such cases, suffering itself becomes a good to be attained. Man always acts in order to obtain some good; to choose evil is impossible. Summing up Dostoyevsky's discussion of the determinism of human conduct: he achieves his purpose to a limited extent, i.e., he demonstrates quite convincingly that utilitarianism in its narrow sense cannot be right, for man often acts against his own practical, material, direct benefit.

But he must let the reader in on another secret: he does not believe a word of what he was written up to now. Or rather, he believes it in a way, but at the same time he suspects that he is "lying like a cobbler."

Comment

Dostoyevsky in the first part of *Notes from Underground* pushed sincerity to its utmost limits. His literary objective had been "to tell the truth" from his earliest youth. Already in a letter dated August 16, 1839, addressed to his brother, Michael, he vowed to "get to the bottom of the mystery of the human personality." From a modern point of view *Notes* is his most daring, his most experimental work. As a literary ideal, sincerity has gained increasing momentum since Dostoyevsky's lifetime. It became the object of a cult on the part of Andre Gide (1869-1951), one of Dostoyevsky's most fervent admirers. Taking the production of the first half of the twentieth century as a whole, one would be tempted to assert that this cult was the most powerful literary inspiration of the period. When the narrator divulges that he is skeptical of the truth of what he has written he actually achieves the utmost in truthfulness, for a question about the accuracy of the statement must always be present in the subject when he deals with human consciousness and its states.

Each man has memories that he would tell only to some of his friends. There are other things that he would only reveal to himself. But each man has reminiscences that he would be afraid to tell even to himself. The underground man will now try to recall some of his early memories that he has always avoided, to see whether one can be perfectly truthful to oneself. Heine states that a true autobiography is impossible to write, because we are bound to lie about ourselves. He claims that probably even Rousseau was mendacious in his *Confessions*. But Heine was talking about literary endeavors that were meant to be read, whereas the underground man writes for himself only. But then, why does he constantly refer to the reader? Why does he put his thoughts on paper at all? Perhaps because it is more impressive to imagine that one has an audience. Or perhaps he will be relieved by the writing. He will get rid of some of these unpleasant memories.

Comment

The first part of the *Notes* dealt with the inner life, and there the great question was whether man can be sincere, that is, whether he can reveal with objectivity what goes on in his mind. The answer was largely negative, as we have seen. Now the underground man turns to external reality to see whether the truth, notably that aspect of the truth that everyone is always silent about, can be told. This experiment will comprise Part 2 of the *Notes*. Dostoyevsky considered himself a realist, but he believed that he far surpassed the realists of his time to the extent that he suggested the contradictions, the irrationality, the vast resources of the human personality. He was not interested, he said, in banal, everyday occurrences, whose existence is neither questioned nor denied by anyone. The task of the true writer is to reveal the hidden side of reality. Thus, like many authors coming after him, he conceived of literature as exploration. It is also worth noting that he recognized the therapeutic qualities of writing. Lastly, let us mention that Rousseau's *Confessions* is very much to the point here. The greatest figure of French pre-romanticism, Rousseau, intended to pull no punches, to hide nothing in his confessions. The underground man's aim is of course to do better than Rousseau.

NOTES FROM THE UNDERGROUND

TEXTUAL ANALYSIS

PART 2: APROPOS OF THE WET SNOW

....

The second part is so titled for the simple reason that it was snowing when the underground man started to compose it. It has for its motto a poem by Nekrassov about the anguish of "memories of foul disgrace." The underground man was then twenty-four. His life was similar to what it is now in its gloom and loneliness. He made no friends at the office. His colleagues, he imagined, looked upon him with loathing. He often wondered why the others never thought they were disliked. One clerk had a pock-marked face, another wore a uniform so ancient that it smelled. But they were not disturbed by thoughts of being repulsive, or if they had known they were disliked they would not have minded. Now he believes that he hated himself and projected his feelings into the others. He fancied that others had the same attitude towards him as he did toward himself. In turn, he heartily detested the other clerks. At the same time, he was afraid of them. He could not face them. He used to try whether he could stand the gaze of a certain colleague. The underground man was always the first to avert his gaze. He dreaded seeming ridiculous, too. He therefore meticulously observed the conventional forms in external things. He prided himself on his intelligence, yet he tried to avoid any show of eccentricity. He was morbidly sensitive.

Comment

These introductory remarks contain many acute observations as well as insights. It is interesting to note that practically all the points Dostoyevsky made have since become the concern of new schools in literature, philosophy, psychology, and sociology. One cannot say that the author's influence brought them into the spotlight of interest - *Notes from Underground* has not been one of Dostoyevsky's best-known works until recently - rather, he anticipated certain trends that were implicit in the development of mankind.

The idea of digging up unpleasant memories has become the foundation of psychoanalysis. Dostoyevsky does not have in mind exactly what Freud meant by repression, though. These reminiscences, he claims, are consciously pushed away. He approximates rather the existentialist doctrine of bad faith. The second important consideration is the notion of alienation. In the *Notes* this is the condition of the intellectual who has been uprooted, who lacks the peasants' firm ethnic integration. Parallel with this is the alienation of urban man in general, the product of the machine age, a notion stressed by Marx, who was Dostoyevsky's contemporary. Another interesting observation refers to projection, an axial notion in modern psychology. Sartre maintains that all we consider to be evil is simply the projection of the unacknowledged part of our personality into others. A further remark worth noting concerns the underground man's sheepish desire to conform, so that he will not be conspicuous. This coexists or alternates in him with the ambition to be intelligent, to be different. Finally, let us point out that Dostoyevsky here attributes his various difficulties to his sensitivity. By sensitivity he means here something akin to what he previously termed acute consciousness, though it has to do with both physical and mental qualities.

All his colleagues were stupid, and resembled one another to perfection. The underground man was the only one who knew he was a coward, just because he was more highly developed. All decent men should be cowards. Only blockheads are brave. He was worried by the knowledge of being unlike anyone else. Now he realizes that this feeling was due to his youth. He had other impulses regarding his relationship with his colleagues. On some occasions he would contemplate making friends with them. Perhaps he scorned them only out of romantic notions he learned from books.

Comment

Why does he say that cowardice must be a characteristic trait of all decent people? The man who realizes his responsibility as well as all the possible evil consequences of his action always hesitates to commit himself. Here intellectuality is represented as a moral quality. As for the statement that the feeling of his "otherness" could be ascribed to his youthful inexperience, this is an additional cause contributing to his alienation, but not a decisive factor by itself. The mention of romantic attitudes emphasizes the literary inspiration of much that he does. The underground man is wrapped up in books, theories, thoughts: this is part of his curse. The Romantics always considered the artistic soul as standing apart from society. Was bookishness really the cause of Dostoyevsky's own alienation? One would rather suspect that he buried himself in books because he was an outcast, or different, or morbidly sensitive. His reading may in turn have reinforced his aloneness and otherness.

He spent most of his time at home, reading. Books helped - he discovered new worlds through them. But at times he was unspeakably bored with them, and he needed some movement, some activity. He plunged into petty, disgusting vices. He indulged in them furtively at night, shamefacedly. Then he would have hysterical convulsions. He dreaded being recognized. He visited various dubious establishments.

Comment

The vices referred to were undoubtedly sexual in nature, involving masturbation and visits to bordellos, with consequent remorse, disgust, and further estrangement from recognized society. The "hysterical convulsions" probably are a reference to Dostoyevsky's epilepsy. If so, it is remarkable that he realized their psychological origin.

One solitary night, as he was walking by a tavern, the underground man saw through the window some men fighting with billiard cues. One man was hurled out of the window. The underground man would have liked to have been dealt with in that way. He went in, hoping that there might be another argument and he would be thrown out. A tall officer put him in his place right away. He stood in the officer's way by the billiard table. The officer moved him away as one would move an object, passing by as though he had not even noticed it. He could have forgiven if the officer had struck him, but to be treated like a fly he could not forgive. He would have liked to start an argument, yet he beat a fast retreat. The next evening he again passed in front of the tavern, but he could not bring himself to walk in and start a quarrel that time either. This was not because he was a coward at heart. He was, though, invariably a coward in action. He was not afraid of pain or violence. He would have positively welcomed the idea of being maltreated. But he dreaded cutting a ridiculous figure. A point of honor was at stake, and in order to talk of a point of honor one has to use literary language. And he was convinced that the moment he would start speaking in lofty terms the whole room, down to the lowest attendant, would split their sides with laughter, and the officer would good-naturedly kick him round the billiard table, and only then might he perhaps condescend to pick him up and drop him out of the window.

Comment

The incident described is in all likelihood substantially taken from the author's life. Seeing that it recounts a very humiliating personal experience, the detachment with which Dostoyevsky looks at himself is certainly striking. This type of retrospective objectivity in personal matters is present in many Russian writers. It may have something to do with another pastime particularly favored by Russians: public self-confession. To speak of himself as a foul, contemptible creature had great attraction for Dostoyevsky. The masochistic nature of his desire to be thrown out of the window is similarly manifest.

The incident left a lasting mark on the underground man's ego. Sometimes he would meet the officer on the street. As the years passed, his hatred even increased and he began to make enquiries about the officer. He learned his name. He followed him to his apartment house to find out where he lived. Then the idea struck him to write a satirical novel with the officer cast as the **protagonist**. He exposed the bestial cruelty of the man. But the novel was not published. He was bristling with resentment. He composed a masterful letter to him, begging him to apologize and hinting that otherwise a duel would have to be fought. It was so nobly written that anyone with the slightest comprehension of what is good and beautiful would have felt compelled to fling his arms around the neck of its author, offering his undying friendship. And how the underground man would have wished it so. But, fortunately he never mailed the letter. Cold shivers run down his spine when he even thinks of what would have happened had he posted this imbecility.

On holidays the underground man was in the habit of strolling down Nevsky Prospect in the afternoon hours.

Comment

Nevsky Prospect was the Fifth Avenue of Saint Petersburg, where the cream of society would promenade on Sundays and holidays.

Why he did this, he cannot say; for this "stroll" was but a series of humiliations. He positively used to wriggle about like an eel, stepping aside to make way for generals, officers of the Guard, and fine ladies. He was acutely conscious of the shabbiness of his appearance, the pitiful abjectness of his scurrying figure. It was a calvary, a martyrdom, an intolerable humiliation. Yet he was drawn to the Nevsky as a fly is to the flypaper; he was indeed treated like an insect by everyone - a highly developed and refined bug, but a bug nevertheless. The officer used to go there quite often himself. Just like the underground man, he too would cower before the high and mighty, but he walked over people whose status was lower than his own, never even turning his head. And every time they met, the underground man stepped aside, though hysterical with rage. He wondered himself why he was doing it. After all, there was no law saying that he should make way: theoretically they were equals. At last he made up his mind that he would not step aside, no matter what happened. But for this he needed a plan. Shabby as he looked, he would never muster up the necessary courage. He therefore acquired a pair of black gloves, and a good hat. He bought an expensive shirt. His overcoat was still holding him back: it was presentable, but it had a cheap raccoon collar. He had to change this to a beaver one, such as is worn by officers. He sold the raccoon collar and decided to borrow the rest of the money from Anton Antonich, his superior. For nights beforehand he could not sleep because of nervousness. He had sudden palpitations. Anton Antonich, though displeased, lent him the money. He now had the required outfit, yet several times he still missed his cue. Once, he stumbled in his excitement and fell. The officer stepped over him. He then abandoned his plan, but for a last time went to the Nevsky just to see how things would turn out. Suddenly, three yards from the enemy, he made the decision to stand fast, closed his eyes, and then went straight for his target. He did not budge an inch, nudging his adversary away as much as the other was pushing him. That evening he returned home elated, triumphant, singing operatic arias.

Comment

The passage above perfectly illustrates Dostoyevsky's anti-bourgeois, anti-establishment sentiments. It shows him as one of the "insulted and injured." The officer's behavior very amply suggests how those of an intermediate social status must bend to their superiors, and give vent to their pent-up aggressiveness only when encountering those below them. The underground man is not presented as an active rebel. Often he blames himself, often no one in particular. He loathes crude and aggressive people - the bourgeoisie, the powerful - especially when they arrogate rights of superhumanity to themselves. But the author does not represent him as realistically planning to take any action, or even making a gesture against his enemies. It must be pointed out that his "revenge" on the officer involved the acquisition of conventional status symbols. On the whole, his reaction to society is completely negative: he withdraws to what he calls his hole, in shame and hurt pride, though objectively he knows his very pride is just playacting. While the underground man is always aware of the falsehood and absurdity of his own position, he takes others for granted, almost never questioning the "naturalness" and genuineness of his fellow men. He labels others as peasants and thereby sacrosanct, or men of action, direct men who are authentic.

His periods of dissipation would alternate with periods of remorse and distaste. But he had another means of escape, a terrain where everything could be reconciled, a refuge where the good and the beautiful reigned forever: daydreaming. He would sometimes dream for three months on end in his corner. In his dreams he became a hero. These dreams were particularly sweet and soothing after one of his bouts. While in real life he was the lowest wretch, in his imagination he became the exact opposite. At times these visions came even during days of dissipation. They did not make him stop the debauchery. On the contrary, they added flavor to it, they gave a certain piquancy and significance to the ugliest excesses. In his dreams he was possessed by a sense of universal love and brotherhood, though in the concrete he never applied this to people. Everything was given a satisfactory, golden, poetic appearance, largely stolen from literary works. Everyone was forced to recognize his superiority, and he forgave them for their past stupidity. He inherited millions and devoted them to the benefit of humanity; he confessed before all his past sins, which, however, were not mere vices but had something beautiful and touching about them. People would kiss him, weeping, while he would walk barefoot and hungry, preaching ideas that would redeem the rottenness in the world. Universal amnesty would be declared while the band would be playing a march. The Pope would agree to abdicate and retire to Brazil. Then there would be a magnificent ball at the Villa Borghese. Lake Como would be transferred for the occasion to Rome.

Comment

Dostoyevsky wishes to suggest that idealism and vice can coexist. Indeed, they admirably complement each other in life. This is a very cynical comment on man's character, for it virtually excludes the possibility of improvement. Another sour observation is that the underground man is full of love for humanity in the abstract but actually he hates almost all of the people he comes into contact with. This is the purport of Sartre's famous passage on humanists in *Nausea:* they love mankind per se, but loathe people individually. The nature of the daydreams brings to mind Bloom, in James Joyce's *Ulysses.* The abdication of the Pope reflects Dostoyevsky's orthodox pan-Russianism. These daydreams are of course presented ironically. *The Notes* implicitly discredits many of the characters in Dostoyevsky's other novels. These are often presented as heroes, but in the present light become more than questionable. The author's lucidity and sincerity are at their highest in the present work, and this among other things explains the growing regard for *Notes from Underground*. Yet we should not conclude that the author here rejects all his ideas of world-redemption and brotherhood. The underground man has only petty vices, and all his positive, constructive impulses have been stifled by society. His humanism has to be relegated to the realm of the imagination, because he finds people too stupid to understand him. He has not chosen the underground out of preference, but has been chased there by the insensitivity, aggressiveness, coarseness, and obtuseness of others. But, it would seem, his unrelieved series of bad experiences has developed a perverse enjoyment of suffering in him and now he has a strange affection for his underground home.

After a couple of months of daydreaming, the underground man would always surface in order to embrace his fellows; and to do this he usually paid a visit to his superior at the office, Anton Antonich Syetochkin, his only permanent acquaintance. Anton Antonich received on Tuesdays, and so the desire to embrace humanity had to be deferred to Tuesdays. The host would talk about excise taxes and promotions with his friends, while the underground man would be sitting there, not knowing what to say, until he became dazed and bade good-bye to the company. This would quell his thirst for mankind for another three months or so.

He had, however, one other acquaintance, a former schoolmate, by the name of Simonov. He had in fact other former classmates living in Saint Petersburg, but he avoided their company for they reminded him of the detestable years of slavery spent at his alma mater. Simonov was different, though. He had a certain honesty. At one time they had a warm relationship, but this did not last long. The underground man suspected that Simonov was now embarrassed by the reminiscence of the times they spent together, fearing that the underground man might again take up the same tone. Though he sensed that Simonov now disliked him, the underground man nevertheless went to see him one afternoon. By the time he was at the door he knew this was a mistake, but he had a compulsion for doing the wrong thing, and he went in.

He found him in an animated conversation with two other former schoolmates. They took almost no notice of the underground man. He realized that they must despise him for his lack of success in the service and for letting himself go in other ways. Simonov seemed surprised to see him. All this was disconcerting, and the underground man sat down, feeling befuddled, unsure of himself. They were planning a farewell dinner in the honor of Zverkov, another common acquaintance, who was going away to a distant province. The underground man knew Zverkov well. In the lower grades he was a pretty, cheerful boy, liked by everybody. He never cared for studies, yet he graduated with good marks, because he had influential relatives. Toward the end of his school career he inherited an estate, which made him boastful. He was a vulgar but good-natured fellow, admired by the others for his wealth and for his reputation of savoir-faire. He had a handsome, stupid face and free-and-easy military manners. It was particularly in the last year of school that the underground man began to hate him. He talked of his future conquests among the fair sex, of duels he was to fight. He swore that he would not leave a single village girl on his estate unmolested. The underground man berated him for this statement, and for once got the better of him. But Zverkov, who had no malice, was always friendly with the underground man when they met, that is, he was until it became evident that the underground man was not advancing in the service, at which time he started to cut him even on the street.

As for the other two present, Ferfichkin was a Russianized German, with a monkey face; a bitter enemy ever since the lower grades and one of Zverkov's toadies. Trudolyubov was a tall young man. He had an open nature, but could only think in terms of promotion. They were now concluding their deliberations, having agreed to meet the next day at the Hotel de Paris, paying seven rubles each. The underground man abruptly suggested that he would chip in too. Simonov, who knew full well that the underground man would have a beastly time were he to go, tried to dissuade him, but accepted. Ferfichkin and Trudolyubov left, and Simonov excused himself, claiming to have made a previous appointment.

Back on the street, the underground man cursed himself for offering to join them, and to celebrate a pig like Zverkov to boot! Besides, he had only nine rubles left and he owed his servant seven rubles for his monthly wages. But he knew he would go. That night he saw the most hideous nightmares. This was only to be expected, since the meeting brought back to mind his miserable school years. A lonely, silent boy, he was sent to boarding school by relatives. He was already apprehensive and timid. His new schoolmates met him with gibes because he was different. He reacted by withdrawing in wounded pride. They said that his face was ugly, yet what stupid faces they had themselves. As a matter of fact, at that school the students seemed physically to degenerate. Many fine-looking boys came there, but in a few years they became repulsive. Because they took no interest in the humanities, indeed in anything serious and important, the narrator regarded them as inferior. They mocked everything that was oppressed or officially looked down upon, even if it was just and true. Rank and status were their gods. He hated them and he was repaid in kind. By this time, he did not even ask for their affection, but he excelled in his studies and this impressed them. He could read books that they did not understand. They tried to brush all this off with sarcasms. When the teachers began to notice his intellectual superiority, the railing ceased but hostility persisted. The underground man felt very lonely. He tried to make advances to a few other students, but his friendship with them was always strained. He did, however, succeed once in making a true friend. But by then he had become a tyrant at heart and he wanted to exercise absolute authority over his friend. He required him to reject all his surroundings, everyone except the underground man. He frightened this friend with his passionate affection: he reduced him to tears. But when the friend became completely devoted to him, the underground man suddenly repulsed him, as though all he had wanted was to subjugate the boy. After his graduation the underground man broke practically all ties to forget about the despised institution.

Comment

The flashback to adolescence provides an important aid to the understanding of Dostoyevsky's personality. The critics agree that it is almost entirely autobiographical. He was already forlorn and distrustful when he was sent to boarding school. The school described here is probably a compound of the Moscow boarding school and the Saint Petersburg engineering academy which he started to attend at age seventeen, a year after his mother's death. He hints that his difficulties had already commenced in the home - we know that the atmosphere there was tense, that he abhorred his father. The next we learn is that his schoolmates' response to him was immediately a negative one; and the explanation given is that he was "not like any of them." This is to be taken partly in the physical sense; he was clumsy, he asserts, and they found even his face ridiculous. But it must also be meant spiritually: he was sensitive, thoughtful, inclined to mental rather than physical activity. His interest in reading developed somewhat later. It seems rather clear that his hatred of them was a reaction, and his excellence in studies a way to get back, to prove that he was as good as any of them.

And here there is another enigmatic reference to his desire to be humiliated by them, which is contradicted by many other statements which show him as possessing great pride, a desire to surpass all others, the inclination to be a tyrant. However, we have to take Dostoyevsky's word that masochistic tendencies, the wish to be punished and humiliated, really existed in him, and that these contradictions were part and parcel of his complex personality. He speaks of his comrades with disgust, but he is not lenient on himself either; he says, "perhaps I was worse than any of them." His most devastating self-criticism is contained in the short passage about the only true friend he ever had, whom he started to hate as soon as he had mentally subjugated him. This is an admission that actually there was no solution to his problems and that the differences between him and his classmates were superficial rather than qualitative.

The next day he stole home from the office two hours early. There were thousands of details to go over. He found all his clothes threadbare. He had visions of how Zverkov would look down upon him. But at the same time he hoped to impress the company with his great wit and spirit. Zverkov would be isolated. The others would be enthralled by the underground man's scintillating words. Finally, they would all be reconciled and drink to their everlasting friendship. He watched the clock nearing the appointed hour with febrile excitement. He hailed a sledge and drove up to the Hotel de Paris in grand style.

He was afraid that he would be the first to arrive. Not only was he first, but the table had not even been laid and he was informed that the dinner had been ordered for six instead of five o'clock. Fuming with indignation, he told himself that the others should have let him know about the change. He sat down and watched the waiter putting on the silver. He could hear laughter and shrieks from the adjoining room. The situation was sickening and he was glad to see Zverkov advance with his friends punctually at six. Zverkov shook hands with him in a friendly manner, with the courtesy of someone wishing to ward off a petitioner.

The underground man had expected him to start laughing and swaggering right away, and his condescending smile disconcerted him. Was this formality meant to be an offense? Or did this fathead Zverkov think that he was so superior he could only look at the underground man in a patronizing way? Zverkov presently expressed surprise that the underground man wanted to join them. He seemed to avoid his old friends, Zverkov continued, and this was regrettable. They learned that he had been waiting for an hour. Zverkov thought this extremely funny, but he tried to hide his hilarity. Ferfichkin giggled. They blamed Simonov, who protested that he did not have the underground man's address. They sat down. Zverkov sat opposite the underground man. He noticed that the underground man was embarrassed and tried to put him at ease. He asked him questions. Why did the underground man quit his previous job? What was his salary? But his questions were not of much help, for each of them implied his superior position over the narrator. Dismayed, the underground man asked if Zverkov was trying to cross-examine him. Yet foolishly he told Zverkov what his yearly income was. A pitiful sum, Zverkov thought; and he added that the narrator looked thin. Zverkov looked at his former classmate's shabby clothes. There was a yellow stain on the underground man's trousers. Blushing, the narrator declared that he was dining here at his own expense. But he was told not to ruin the good mood of the others; after all, no one invited him.

Zverkov now started on one of his stories about how he nearly got married the other day. His tale was adorned with a collection of generals, colonels, and other notables. Simonov and Trudolyubov laughed. No one paid any attention to the underground man. He sat there, humiliated, thinking of how out of place he was among these brutes. He must get up this very minute, he thought, and walk out without a word. But he stayed. He downed glassfuls of sherry and Lafitte. Not being used to alcoholic beverages, it soon went into his head. He hoped to insult them in the most flagrant manner and then go, leaving them with the impression that he was absurd yet a very clever fellow. Zverkov had now started another story, about a lady whom he made declare her love to him. Again he was name dropping, mentioning this time an intimate friend of his, Prince Kolya. At this the narrator suddenly cut in, inquiring impudently why Prince Kolya, who was such a crony of his, did not put in an appearance tonight. This silenced them for a minute. Zverkov examined him, with a detached expression, as one would look at an insect.

The others raised their glasses to drink to Zverkov's health. The narrator sat motionless. Trudolyubov asked him indignantly if he was going to drink too. The underground man answered that he wanted to make a speech first. This idea had just struck him and he did not know what he was going to say. He began by declaring that he hated **cliches** and people who used them, as well as men wearing corsets (presumably Zverkov, who was a bit corpulent, was wearing one). Then he went on to say that he detested obscene and vulgar language and people who used it. He loved truth, justice, honesty, thought; he loved true friendship, on an equal footing. Nevertheless, he concluded, he would drink to Monsieur Zverkov's health. He bade Zverkov seduce the Circassian girls and defend the country. Zverkov, hurt to the quick, stood up and thanked him for his gracious words. The others made menacing remarks, but Zverkov would have none of this. He said he needed no violence to show how much store he set by the narrator's words. Waiting for some miracle to happen, the underground man still stayed. He tried to prove to himself that he would do the others a favor by leaving. He paid his money and so he would sit and drink.

Zverkov moved from the table to the sofa by the wall. He ordered champagne. Trudolyubov, Simonov, and Ferfichkin sat around him, listening to him reverently. The underground man wondered what it was they found stimulating in Zverkov's conversation. They were evidently fond of him. They talked of the Caucasus, of advancement, of financial matters, of Shakespeare's immortality. The narrator, who was not invited to join them, started pacing back and forth on the other side of the room, smiling contemptuously and trying to show that he could not have cared less whether they paid any attention to him. Yet he purposely made a thumping noise with his boots. And from eight until eleven o'clock at night, he kept walking up and down between the table and the fireplace like a fool, telling himself all the while that he was doing as he pleased. At last he became giddy from turning round so many times. He was in agony, sweating and shivering, realizing that in twenty and forty years' time he would still remember his humiliation and ridiculousness. And yet what a fine and cultivated man he was, he thought to himself at moments, how infinitely better than these boors! It was then that Zverkov made his remark about Shakespeare. The underground man suddenly uttered a shrill laugh, but in such an affected and contemptible fashion that the others stopped their conversation and for two minutes sat watching him pace up and down between table and fireplace as one bereft of sanity.

At eleven Zverkov rose, declaring it was time to pay a visit to his favorite house of prostitution. The narrator, his hair soaked with perspiration, exhausted and delirious, walked up to Zverkov and asked for his forgiveness. He insulted everyone, he said, and he was sorry he did it. Zverkov disagreed. Insult him? A creature like the underground man? It was impossible for someone like him to insult a Zverkov. And presently he started for the door, claiming Olympia (one of the girls in the brothel) for himself. The underground man turned to Simonov who stayed behind to tip the waiters. He asked Simonov to lend him six rubles. Simonov stared at him in amazement. Did he want to go with them? The narrator said he did. Simonov first claimed he had no money on him, but upon his continued entreaties took out six rubles and practically threw them in the underground man's face, and ran to overtake his friends. Weeping, the narrator swore he would make them want his friendship or would slap Zverkov in the face.

Comment

With its minutely described psychological details, its tragicomic tone, and merciless lucidity of analysis, this dinner comprises a minor masterpiece. The underground man was meant to be funny, yet the hopeless horror of the situation comes through too. Every word said, every gesture is verisimilar, convincing. It apparently had a basis in reality; the author's imagination provided the rest, filling out the eventual gaps in his memory. Again it shows Dostoyevsky's feverish sensitivity. In all likelihood he exaggerated his own absurdity as well as the contempt of the others toward him. But it is equally clear that subjectively the incident is a faithful transcription of experience: perhaps it was all in the narrator's mind, but this was the way he felt. In the end he wants to go with the company because he is still clutching to the hope of proving himself before the others.

Rushing down the stairs, the underground man bitterly reflected on the difference between the Pope's leaving Rome for Brazil and the reality of the adventure he had to face that day. But, talking to himself, he said he was a rascal if he dared to laugh at this. Then, assuring himself, he concluded that it all did not matter; everything was lost anyway. Out on the street he caught sight of a low-class sleigh. He jumped in, but at that instant the memory of how Simonov handed him the six rubles made him double up and he collapsed into the sleigh like an empty bag.

Comment

One excellent little touch in this paragraph is the narrator's argument with himself. In the original, it is more like an internal monologue, with syntactical distortions resembling the thought process. Most significantly, it suggests the dichotomy of the self. Another illuminating flash is the way he doubles up thinking of the loan of rubles. None of these observations would be particularly striking in a book written today, but in Dostoyevsky's day minute and revealing details of this sort were still new.

Seated in the sleigh, he made up his mind that he would show them now or he would perish. He rather doubted that they would beg for his friendship; thus the only alternative was to slap Zverkov. They were going to be in the drawing room. Olympia would be sitting with Zverkov on the sofa. Damnable Olympia, she refused to have anything to do with the underground man just the other day. He would pull her hair and pull Zverkov by one ear around the room. They would be sure to beat up the narrator, though. So what? He would strike first, the first slap would be his; that is all that counts according to the laws of honor. There would be a duel, that was for certain. But where was he to get pistols? And powder? And bullets? How could everything be arranged by day-break? Oh well, it would all turn out some way. But even as he was thinking these things, he had a growing awareness of the absurdity of the whole plan and the other side of the question was getting the upper hand.

Comment

The main virtue of the second part of the *Notes* is that it demonstrates concretely what was asserted abstractly and in generalities in the first part. In the passage just summarized, we see how his doubting, polarized, intellectual self breaks down everything until action becomes impossible. At the same time, of course, Dostoyevsky illustrates the incompatibility of romantic fancy and stark reality.

Would it not be better to go straight home? No, that was out of the question. True enough, he would be thrown out of his job and sent to Siberia. In fifteen years, however, when they would let him out, broken and in rags, he would drag himself to Zverkov's, telling the monster that he had lost everything, including the woman he loved, through Zverkov. He would pull out two pistols. But in the last minute he would forgive the wretched scoundrel and fire his weapon in the air. The underground man was moved to tears as he thought of this noble scene. He was dismayed to remember, though, that it was out of Pushkin's Silvio and Lermontov's Masquerade.

Comment

The underground man is ashamed to admit that he is not spontaneous, not original in his dream. He is trying to make life conform to literature, to images borrowed from his favorite novelists. He sets this up as one of the distinguishing marks of the man "divorced from the soil and the national consciousness." But, after all, those living within an ethnic community set their lives by much more rigid outside patterns than the uprooted intellectuals. As a matter of fact, the very problem the underground man faces is that he lacks the direction a "nature" tradition supplies to country folk.

He again decided for the slapping action and was already thunderstruck by the idea that all the horror it entailed would now have to happen. Arriving, he walked into the drawing room. There was no one there. The company had by now gone to the different private rooms. The madam ushered in a girl with a fresh, young face, large, wondering eyes, and a serious expression. Her gravity appealed to him. She was not beautiful, but well developed. The narrator felt something base stir in him and he walked straight up to her. Besides, he felt an enormous relief that the slapping would not have to take place.

At two a.m. the underground man woke from his slumber. The room he was in had a low ceiling; it was small and cramped with boxes. The candle flickered, it had burned down to a stump. Suddenly the memory of the whole ghastly night came back to him. Indeed, it had been with him all the time, even in his sleep, as a nameless, threatening thing. His head was heavy. Anger welled up in him again. He caught sight of a pair of dark eyes looking at him coldly. They made him shiver. He had not said a single word to this girl, thinking it unnecessary. Now he realized the brutality of his approach. What he performed was the act in which true love should be consummated; without love it is mere vice. He felt uncomfortable under her steady gaze. He asked what her name was. She was called Liza. Where did she come from? From Riga. Her parents were tradespeople. She was twenty. He asked why she had left them. She declined to say. He knew he should leave, but a sickly sensation paralyzed him. He recalled something he had seen the previous morning and told her about it: in the wet snow, two workers were carrying out a coffin from the basement of a house of prostitution.

They almost dropped it. On a day like that there must have been water a foot deep in an open grave at Volkovo cemetery. They must have let her casket down into a filthy marsh. Liza countered with stubborn silence. He elaborated on his story. The corpse was that of a prostitute like Liza. She was in debt to the madam. She was a consumptive. She had to keep working until the end. He heard her story from a couple of sleigh-drivers standing by. They were laughing. The narrator invented most of this as he was going along. Then, addressing himself to Liza, he told her that her lot would be the same. She was still pretty and young. A year hence her looks would be just a little bit tarnished, she would have to go to a less expensive establishment. Then she would slip gradually lower and lower until, in another seven years, she would be in a basement. That is, if she was going to be lucky and not get some ailment.

He was now warming to his subject. He told Liza she was still young, she might get married, and be happy. Any married life would be better than the one she had here. He said she was a slave here. After a time it would be too late to break her chains. She was probably already in debt. She would never buy her freedom back. He reminded her of the way they had just met. They did not say a word to each other. Was this the manner human beings should come together? Was that love? She assented vigorously for the first time. She too thought this hideous. Her receptivity egged him on. She could be influenced, after all. He wanted to test his power of persuasion on her. He tried to approach her feelings from the right angle. He wondered whether sentimentality would work. At the same time, he was genuinely concerned about her. He now stated he did not believe a girl like her would come to such a place at her own will. This caught her, because it put her in a special class. If he had had a home, he continued, he would not have become the wretch that he now was. But his parents died when he was still young. If he had a daughter, he went on, he would love her more than anyone else. He once knew a father who was a coarse and stern man, but he would go down on his knees before his daughter. He would wear rags but he gave his last penny to his daughter. He would never let his daughter marry because he was too jealous. He could not stand the thought of her kissing anyone else. Liza retorted that some men think so little of their daughters that they sell them. Aha, that was her case, the underground man imagined. He was filled with a warm feeling toward her. That sort of thing comes about through poverty, he said aloud.

Then he spoke of the marriage between two people who are in love. Even if there are quarrels, it is sweet to make up after - husband and wife feel new inside, as if they met for the first time. Love is a mystery; and it should be kept as a secret bond. When physical attraction diminishes with the passing of years, the union of souls that follows it is something even more precious. Everything becomes a joy when one knows one does it for a beloved being. As the children grow up, one is reborn in them. And how lovely babies are! Their rosy little cheeks, their miniature nails! He raved on fancying that she was now completely bewitched by the images he conjured up for her. Suddenly he stopped, turning crimson, struck by the idea that perhaps she was going to burst out laughing. He waited for her to say something. "Why do you..." that was all she said. But he could make out from her voice that she was deeply moved. This made him feel guilty. But now her voice changed, it had a ring of **irony**. She told him he spoke just like a book. The underground man was furious, not realizing that she was merely hiding her emotions behind the cloak of **irony**, as truly chaste people often do.

Comment

Liza belongs to Dostoyevsky's favorite type of woman character. She is shy, downtrodden, meek, and an aura of sadness crowns her youth. It is this gravity that particularly appeals to him. The great French romantic poet, Baudelaire, one of the precursors of symbolism, asserted for the first time that sadness is of the essence of beauty. Sadness was among Dostoyevsky's aesthetic criteria, too.

The powerfully presented burial scene of the little prostitute effectively underlines the keynote of the second part of the *Notes:* wet snow, moldiness, gloom, darkness. All represent the narrator's moral decay, the spiritual underground in which he lives, devoid of human relationships. He himself is dead, in a manner of speaking. If one takes activity as the measure of life his underground is Hades, the underworld, a kind of spiritual limbo, from which he is too weak and too deeply wounded to escape. This notion of a life that is the equivalent of death was one of the main literary themes of the Romantics. In the sense Dostoyevsky meant it the concept is modern. It can be traced in contemporary poets and novelists such as Jean Genet and William Burroughs. Delivering a religious sermon while lying in bed with a prostitute is certainly a grotesque undertaking. The narrator is fully aware of this as well as the fact that his very motives are questionable, yet his exhortation contains thoughts that were not discredited by Dostoyevsky. There is truth in what the narrator says, despite all the absurdity.

Now he had an evil desire to bring her to her knees. How could she say he talked like a book? Was it possible she did not see her degeneration herself? Did she think she would never grow old? Even though she was attractive, he felt sick as soon as he came to himself after the act. This was a place where one came only drunk. But in any other place men would perhaps fall in love with her, would not dare touch her with even an impure thought. The lowest laborer was better off than she, for he would not sell both his body and soul. No one wastes love on a girl who can be had without love. Perhaps the madam let her have a lover. But did Liza think a man could really love her in this condition? He would only want her money. Let her try to ask whether he would marry her. He would laugh in her face. Her youth would pass quickly. She would be kicked out. But even before that, the madam would start nagging her, abusing her, and once she would begin to slip, no one would take her side. At twenty-two, she would look like a woman of thirty-five. In no time she would be at the Haymarket (where the cheapest brothels were located). Last New Year's Day he saw a woman at a door there. She had been turned out into the street as a joke, because she had been weeping and wailing. She was disheveled, covered with bruises, and drunk. Cabmen and soldiers were making fun of her. Maybe ten years ago that woman had been brought to this very place as an innocent girl. In fact, it would be regarded as a happy eventuality were Liza to die of consumption. When she would be dying, everyone would abandon her; they would even scold her for taking so long to die. Dying, she would be thrown to the dirtiest corner of the cellar. And then in the grave it would be sleet, filth, wet snow. And there her memory on earth would end.

   The underground man had become so worked up by his own story that he felt like crying. He had been carried away, trying to see whether he could get hold of her decent side. But now he saw that the effect was even beyond his expectations: her chest was heaving, she bit the pillow in order to suppress her sobs. He was panic-stricken. He lit a candle to find his clothes. Liza's face was contorted. He took her hand to soothe her, begging her pardon for saying what he did and asking her to come and pay a visit to him. Liza promised that she would. He was trying to beat a quick retreat, but she said she wanted to show him something. Her features were now gleaming and childish. She handed him a letter. It was a love letter written by a medical student with genuine feeling. It was extremely respectful. She explained that she had been to a party where she met a young man she had known from Riga. He knew nothing about the place she lived at. Three days before he had sent this letter through a friend. She added that she was going to leave the brothel as soon as she paid her debt. The narrator saw that the letter was her pride, her claim to a life she was never to achieve. It would lie in a box, her only treasure, and would lead to nothing. He pressed her hand and left. He already had a glimpse of the truth behind his present exhaustion.

Waking up in the morning, he reproached himself for last night's sentimentality. But his first concern was to dispose of the affair with Zverkov. He borrowed another fifteen rubles from Anton Antonich and upon getting home immediately sat down to write to Simonov. The letter had a candid, fraternal, even humorous tone; it was admirably well written, as all of the underground man's letters. He blamed everything on the effect of the wine, to which he was unaccustomed. He added that he seemed to remember as though in a dream that he insulted Zverkov. He asked them all to forgive him. There was a certain lightness about the way it was put, which suggested that he was slightly amused by the incident and was not going to give it another thought. He felt very satisfied with himself. A cultivated and educated man knows how to extricate himself from an affair like that, he thought. He put six rubles into the envelope and sent off the letter.

He went for a walk, but felt that something was still weighing on his mind. It was Liza. It worried him that she might come. What if she saw the way the underground man lived. Yesterday he could play the hero before her. He looked at his dressing gown, which was in tatters. He would be nervous, as usual, and would crawl and scrape in front of her. And the lies he told her! But no, he was honest, he spoke sincerely. Yet, he was ill at ease. He had before him the image of her face when he had struck a match and saw her distorted expression, that tortured look of hers. Next day, thinking of the eventuality of her coming, he panicked and ran about in the room like a maniac, cursing her sentimental soul. Her head was turned by his artificially concocted, bookish talk. What purity there was in her, what freshness of the soil! But she did not come. After nine o'clock the underground man felt a little calmer, for he thought she could not come later than nine. He was beginning to have daydreams about her. He became Liza's rescuer. He educated her. She developed into a fine, intelligent woman. One day she flung herself at his feet, declaring her undying love. But he was forced to admit that he borrowed this idea from George Sand.

This was the period of the narrator's monthly battle over Apollon's wages. He hated Apollon possibly more than anyone else on earth. The man's self-assurance, conceit, and arrogance were intolerable. He was always attempting to reduce Apollon to obedience and humility by withholding his wages and making him beg for them. But Apollon had his proven strategy for extricating the money without humbling himself. He would come into the room every two hours and look at the narrator with utter contempt. If asked what the matter was, he would say nothing, but turn around with a most significant air. Should this routine fail to work, he had a last resort, which was to sigh while gazing at the underground man, making no comment, but apparently appalled by his moral degradation. As things stood, Apollon was still applying his first routine, but the underground man, unhinged by his recent experiences, could not stand it, flew into a rage, and called Apollon his torturer. Apollon for his part assured him that he could report him at the police for insulting behavior, and left the room. The narrator charged after him, and invited him to call the police. While he was shrieking hysterically at Apollon, the door opened. It was Liza. Swooning with shame, the narrator rushed back into his room and started to tear at his hair in confusion. But Apollon appeared two minutes later, announcing that a woman wanted to see the underground man. Liza walked in.

Comment

The narrator's feelings, his dread of seeing Liza again, are complex. He has realized that the girl is important to him. He knows that with his rhetoric of the other day he has succeeded in winning her respect and admiration. But just because she is important, he is afraid of ruining the effect, shattering the first impression. He is ashamed of his poverty because it is the wrong setting for a scene in a romantic opera. Furthermore, he understands that after the high-flown speech he delivered to her everything would be an anticlimax. Finally, he has a bad conscience over his lack of sincerity. What he told her was essentially the truth, and if it was going to change her life it would certainly be for the better. Yet he did it partly to prove his power, his skill of persuasion, and he elaborated on the beauties of married life to satisfy his poetic fancy. The burden that is weighing on him is the burden of responsibility. Objectively, he is no more meretricious than most people, but his sensitive conscience, his self-doubting, analytical mind make him see himself as a fake. Again, he is conscious of playing a game. But now a human life depends on the machinations that, it seems to him, he resorts to in order to chase away his boredom. Others must pay for the flights of his imagination. He conceives of Liza as a simple, trusting product of the soil whom he is corrupting. She represents the purity and innocence of the Russian masses to him.

Dejected, he stood before her, under Apollon's stern gaze. At last Apollon left, but this did not help his embarrassment. To make things worse, she seemed confused too. Gradually his shame was turning into rage at the humiliation he had been subjected to and dimly he was already conscious of a voice demanding vengeance on her. He said she should not imagine he was ashamed of his poverty. On the contrary, he was proud of it. He ran to Apollon just to be out of the room, entreated him to go get some tea and biscuits. He gave Apollon his wages. The servant consented. But now the narrator had to face Liza again. On his way back he was toying with the idea of running away as he was, in his dressing gown. Neither of them could speak for a couple of minutes. Suddenly he shouted, "I'll kill him!" He meant Apollon. Then he burst into tears. It was a hysterical attack. He asked in a soft and sickly voice for water. Actually, he did not need water, nor did he feel faint, but this was good for a little interlude. Apollon brought the tea. It seemed to the narrator that this tea was terribly commonplace. Blushing, he asked Liza if she despised him. As she was too confused to answer, he commanded her angrily to drink her tea. He knew that she was not to blame for anything, yet he became more and more furious. He decided he was not going to speak at all, in order to punish her. At the same time, he realized this was both a mean and stupid thing to do. Finally she blurted out that she wanted to leave "that place" altogether.

Now he was ready to answer. She came to him because he had given her a sentimental speech. But, he continued, he was laughing inside all the while. He had gone to the bordello to avenge himself on an officer. He could not find Zverkov and so he had to vent his spleen on someone else. He wanted to humiliate her because he himself had been humiliated. He wanted to make her cry. He hated her even then because of the lies he was telling. He just likes to play with words, and he wants to be left alone. He knew he was a scoundrel and a sluggard. He had been dreading that she might come for the last three days. What worried him especially was that he had posed as a hero to her and that now she would see his poverty. He would never forgive her for finding him in a tattered dressing gown, and at the moment he was shrieking at Apollon, to boot. He would never forgive her for confessing this either. While he admits to being the nastiest rat on earth, he is no worse than all the others, the difference being that they are never embarrassed, while it is his lot to always be insulted by every louse. But his tirade did not repulse Liza the way he thought it would. She understood a great deal; at least, she saw that he was miserable. She held out her hand in friendship, she threw her arms around the narrator and started sobbing. He could not restrain himself either but burst into tears too. "I can't be good…they won't let me!" he whined, and he went on crying for another quarter of an hour. But after a while he began to feel uncomfortable lying face down on the sofa. He was ashamed to raise his head and look at her. He realized that their parts had changed and that now he was the downtrodden victim and she was the heroine. But, when he finally got up enough courage to raise his head, suddenly a different impulse overtook him, an impulse for mastery and possession. It resembled an act of vengeance. He gripped her hands passionately and she warmly embraced him.

Fifteen minutes later the underground man was pacing back and forth in the room like a caged tiger. Every now and then he peeped through the screen to see if Liza was at last going. She was sitting on the floor. She must have been crying. This time she understood everything. He had finally succeeded in insulting her. She now knew that he was a despicable man and that he was incapable of love. With him loving meant being a tyrant, love was a struggle, the will to subjugate. Afterwards, he no longer needed the defiled object. From the depth of his depravity he could not even comprehend the tender, self-sacrificing love with which she had come to him. He was just insufferably oppressed by her presence. She made him so nervous that he could not bear her presence another minute. He went up to her and thrust a five-ruble note in her hand. He did this purposely to offend her even more. This evil act was a product of his brain, it was taken from books. But as soon as he did it he was sorry. He rushed after her and called her from the staircase. She did not answer. He went back to the room and noticed that the five-ruble note was there on the table. He hastily put on some clothes and ran to the street. He ran about two hundred yards to the crossroads and there he stopped. Why was he going after her? To ask for her forgiveness? But perhaps he would hate her again in another day, just because today he kissed her feet. He could never give her happiness, with his tyrannical tendencies. Now she felt insulted, and this would purify her. Noble suffering is better than cheap happiness.

He has never again heard of Liza. After all these years, her memory is still an open wound in the underground man's heart. What he has written-here is hardly literature, rather it is a kind of self-punishment. He has shown the reader how he spoiled his life by rotting in his hole through divorce from reality. Novels are written around heroes, while he is an anti-hero. The result will produce an unpleasant impression, for people do not like real life. Things are better in books. But the reader should not blame the narrator without first taking a look inside himself. Perhaps it has been only through cowardice if the reader has not carried things so far as the narrator. Perhaps he has more life in him than the reader. People do not even know any more what living means, they would be completely lost without books. We are afraid of the idea of being individuals, we are ashamed of it; we are trying to conform to some sort of generalized man. We are all stillborn, and prefer our shadow lives to reality.

Comment

Towards the end it is more and more the evil side of the narrator's personality that Dostoyevsky emphasizes. The underground man cannot love, because he only wants to subjugate the object of his desires; afterwards, he loses interest. The episode, mentioned earlier in the book, involving a friend from whom the underground man demanded total devotion illustrates this theme. As soon as affection was obtained he no longer cared. With Liza sensual and sexual love are involved in addition to emotional and intellectual matters. The idea of wanting to "have" people, in every sense of the word, instead of giving them steady, affectionate support, is by no means a new one. Dostoyevsky sees it as part of the underground man's sadistic tendencies. This is remarkable, because elsewhere and on repeated occasions, he draws attention to his wish to be punished, to be maltreated, to be abused. That such contradictory dispositions should coexist in one person is not inconceivable and it would be wrong to accuse Dostoyevsky of being inconsistent on this account. However, he does present an unfair picture of the protagonist toward the end when he emphasizes this one feature of his personality almost to the exclusion of all others. To be more exact, it is the underground man who emphasizes it.

But in the entire story it is his high-strung, nervous, morbidly sensitive condition rather than his cynical sybaritism or moral depravity that impresses the reader. He dreaded to have to face Liza again principally because he knew he had somehow created in her a very splendid image of himself, and, being particularly fond of Liza, he did not want this to be shattered. All his brutal and cruel deeds are connected with his feelings of personal inadequacy. His resolution to avenge himself on Liza because of his humiliation strikes one as more stupid than mean. Even the act of sensual brutality that is implied toward the end was brought about by a sense of embarrassment: he simply did not know what to do as a human being, and let the animal in himself take over.

The entire question of moral domination and sexual subjugation is a side issue in the *Notes*, whose main purport is to show a fragmented, disintegrated character, a man in whom the sense of identity itself has become faint, a person refractory to definition. At the conclusion of the book, the author returns to the main theme. In the last paragraph he suddenly sees the underground man move positively. He even sets him up as man who has dared to go farther than most, who has embraced real life as opposed to most people who only live by books. Here he definitely appears to forget that the underground man spends most of his time in total inactivity, withdrawn to his detested hole, reading and dreaming. Adventures such as the one with Liza comprise the exception and not the rule in his life. His one great forte is sincerity. In this one respect he is superior to his fellow men. He faces life as it is, but most of the time he cannot forge ahead from that point.

NOTES FROM THE UNDERGROUND

CHARACTER ANALYSES

THE NARRATOR

The most striking aspect of the narrator's character is that he has none or little of it: he lacks character, and not only in the sense of moral strength and discipline, but also in the wider meaning of nature, self, and personality. Let us, for the last time, explain and summarize why he says this and what he understands by it. Obviously, he has physical characteristics, physiognomy, blood circulation, etc., like any of us. The lack of features is a mental quality. Here we must call the student's attention to an important distinction which must be grasped or the entire concept will be confusing. On the one hand there is no doubt that the underground man has a certain type of face, complexion, a certain height, and so forth, But even his perception of these physical features may be a matter of doubt with him because of his analytical approach. Many of the terms we use to describe the body are comparative, and therefore relative rather than absolute: tall, slender, myopic are words depending on comparisons. Such designations as beautiful or ugly are subjective. Therefore, even on this level the underground man is faced with a difficult task in attempting to define himself. (So is everyone, of course, once he starts to ask questions.)

The second level of difficulty concerns sense perceptions inside the body. A case in point is the underground man's toothache. When it starts, he simply registers it. Sensory perception is of course subjective by its nature, but at first he has no doubt that he is experiencing pain, and that it corresponds to some malfunction or inadequacy in the organism. But as time passes he purposely exaggerates the condition, complaining about it and testing it until he is convinced the toothache itself is a lie he has invented to torture his environment.

The third level is that of the emotions. It is here that the real problem begins. He is capable of experiencing emotions. Sometimes, indeed, he is overwhelmed by his feelings. Before Liza's coming he is gripped by fear. During her visit he alternates between shame and anger. This oscillation between different emotions (fear, shame, anger) caused by one factor, the importance of Liza, indicates Dostoyevsky's awareness that different emotive choices can be made by the individual to solve a potentially threatening situation. The emotive reaction is sometimes there, and there is no question about it in the underground man's mind. More often, though, this certainty is lacking. At such times, his spite is a game, his love is an act, his sentimentality, a sham borrowed from books. What are the main reasons for the want of correspondence? First, it is his high intellectuality. What is semi-conscious or half-instinctive in others is fully cognitive in the underground man. As he sees the two sides of every problem, he cannot commit himself emotionally. Secondly, he disintegrates his emotivity with introspection. As we have pointed out, the emotions evaporate to the extent that we wish to ascertain them. In the third place, he identifies falsely with characters out of books. His personality becomes inextricably entangled with those of his fictional heroes.

Finally, on the level of the intellect, we cannot properly speak of character at all. In fact, the intellect constitutes the underground man's curse, it is the source of all evil. At times he calls a higher form of consciousness a disease. The intellectual, to him, and to Dostoyevsky, is a morbid creature, and an immoral one. This is closely connected with the fact that he is divorced from the community he grew out of. He is alienated. He withdraws to his hole where he escapes into dreams. Yet he has some unusual adventures in real life as well. Only, he is too sensitive and takes things altogether too seriously to participate in social life on a permanent basis. If there is a key to the underground man's character, it is sensitiveness. He has to take reality in small doses, with plenty of time for absorption after each harrowing escapade. Many of the "evil" actions the narrator perpetrates are simply due to nervousness and embarrassment.

There are two other important character traits mentioned in the book, and the narrator expresses no doubt as to their presence in him. These are his masochistic and sadistic tendencies. He claims that he derives pleasure from being insulted. At the same time, however, he suffers severely when he is treated like an "insect" i.e., an object. On other occasions he likes to treat others as objects. This is shown in the way he talks to the petitioners as a clerk, his behavior toward the only true friend he ever had, and his relationship with Liza, who periodically evokes a brutal sensuality from him. The sadistic-masochistic polarity is typical of the underground man's behavior pattern. He has to go through cycles of sin, repentance, abstention, and fall, even though he knows the phases will recur without fail, unending.

ZVERKOV

The underground man regards him with an equal amount of envy and contempt. He has everything the narrator is deficient in or deprived of: money, good looks, social graces, an outgoing personality, success, admiring friends, and women to dote on him. He is a man of action. He never questions anything and never watches himself and thus his hands are not tied. Nor is he restrained by moral considerations. The narrator is sincere enough to admit his envy of Zverkov; on the other hand, his contempt is probably just as genuine. If Zverkov skims life as one glances over a mildly interesting book, he has no true understanding of anything and no real satisfactions.

LIZA

She is the personification of the values associated with the Russian masses and particularly with simple Russian womanhood. Despite her profession, she is pure and innocent. She reminds us of another of Dostoyevsky's heroines, also a prostitute, Sonia in *Crime and Punishment*.

Even before Dostoyevsky it had become fashionable to portray prostitutes as moral giants: Mme. Gautier in *La Dame aux camelias* by Dumas is a case in point. Dostoyevsky reveals the human tragedy behind the surface. It is not the "loose" women we have to blame but society that forces destitute persons into this trade and then throws them unto the wasteheap after they have been worn out. The passage in which the underground man recounts the death of a little prostitute is among the most forceful and moving in the book. One knows that such will indeed be Liza's end too. Much of the underground man's self-hatred centers round the fact that he has been one of those who defiled this innocent creature and that even his speech is out of interested motives.

FERFICHKIN

He is the lowliest person in the novel, a sycophant, and that mainly for financial motives. While the underground man is in many ways a noble failure, Ferfichkin is thoroughly contemptible, having no alleviating circumstances to explain his misdeeds. Dostoyevsky usually reserves to foreigners, namely to Western Europeans, this degree of worthlessness. Ferfichkin is a naturalized Russian of German background. It is possible that his figure is based on one of the author's former classmates, but his portrayal must have also been influenced by Dostoyevsky's impressions during his travels in Germany.

NOTES FROM THE UNDERGROUND

CRITICAL COMMENTARY

When *Notes from Underground* was published in 1864 in the periodical *Epoch*, the immediate critical reaction to it was unfavorable, for it seemed to make fun of ideals then popular with Russian intellectuals. In particular, it was taken as a rebuttal of the conceptions expressed in a novel by Chernyshevsky, *What Is To Be Done?* This had been published about a year before the *Notes*. Critics of Dostoyevsky's work rarely made any mention of *Notes from Underground* before the general spread of the anti-scientific, anti-determinist trend in philosophy and literature, at about the time of Dostoyevsky's death. Before the turn of the century, his star had been eclipsed by his great compatriot, Tolstoy. Nietzsche was among the first to talk of Dostoyevsky in the terms we have been discussing him: he read the *Notes* and recognized in the Russian author a keen psychological insight. Nietzsche asserted that Dostoyevsky was the only author who had taught him anything about the human psyche.

Modern critical thought considers the *Notes* as a turning point in the author's production. Up to their publication, he had never plunged into the depths of consciousness to a similar extent. Nicholas Berdyaev, who wrote two monographs on Dostoyevsky, published in 1922 and 1929, puts this in the following terms: "[in the *Notes*] he becomes a metaphysician, following the tragedy of the human spirit to its very end...." Berdyaev actually means metapsychologist or depth psychologist. Berdyaev already saw the significance of the *Notes* in that they emphasize the irrational side of human nature and its attraction towards lawless freedom and suffering. Man can choose suffering rather than profit. The methods of mathematics do not apply to man. Irrationality is of the essence of life; human society will never obey the norms prescribed by science.

GIDE

Andre Gide recognized the *Notes* not merely as a mark of division but the key to Dostoyevsky's works. In a series of lectures given at the Vieux Colombier for the Dostoyevsky centennial and continued after the centenary celebrations, Gide pointed out that was French critics usually objected to in the Russian author, namely, the irrational, unresolved, and irresponsible behavior of his characters, was in fact Fyodor Dostoyevsky's greatest merit. Of course, as a Frenchman, Gide approached his subject from a French point of view. He called attention to the debt Dostoyevsky evidently owes to Rousseau, but he preferred the Russian's style because of its lack of pathos and mannerisms, its humility. He thought that Dostoyevsky's way of composition is semi-conscious; the artist always gives himself in his works, without precisely knowing who he is. Gide perceptively analyzed the underground man as well as other of Dostoyevsky's main characters and found that emotions in them frequently turn into their opposites. He thought that Dostoyevsky's creations always move on the plane of humility and pride. One should classify them, he argued, on the basis of the amount of pride they possess. The disdainful ones are always the most intellectual.

All in all, intelligence plays a demoniacal part in Dostoyevsky's novels. Even when they are virtuous or strive for virtue, their pride becomes their perdition. Dostoyevsky's heroes can only enter the kingdom of God when they renounce their intelligence and individual will. In this connection Gide justly emphasizes the presumable influence of Schopenhauer. (The German voluntarist philosopher Schopenhauer posited the will as the supreme evil. However, Gide appears to ignore the fact that the German regarded the intellect as will turned against itself.) In his political forecasts Dostoyevsky was wrong with unfailing consistency. The only truths we can learn from him, Gide reminds us, are psychological ones. Although he was not a good theoretician he was a superb observer and recorded.

Gide makes a very interesting comparison between Dostoyevsky's procedure and the method of most French authors. The Frenchman instinctively tries to organize the data at hand. He must present the person he is depicting as a logical, cohesive whole. If he finds that in reality his model diverges from the pattern it should follow, the French novelist will suppress these divergences. Even in life, Gide claims, Frenchmen fashion themselves, their behavior, after an ideal. They behave as they think persons like them should behave. The inconsistencies, the deviations from the norm appear annoying and ridiculous to a Frenchman. Dostoyevsky shows us characters that yield to contradictions. In fact, it is the negations and inconsistencies that interest the Russian author the most. The sphere where these contradictions come into play is the emotions. Dostoyevsky's characters experience emotions that are each other's opposites, almost simultaneously. This is an aspect of the person's duality. But the duality that Dostoyevsky describes is not the pathological split personality of a medical textbook. He espies the contradictions that all of us have inside us, but that we try to deny in order to make ourselves resemble the model. This is disconcerting and downright embarrassing to the Western reader.

The contradictions, Gide says, are most confusing when they appear simultaneously. The Dostoyevskian hero is closest to love when he exaggerates his hatred. We who live on the basis of established conventions are perplexed to find our secret thoughts brought to light in the Russian writer's creations. Gide quotes a famous phrase by Oscar Wilde: it is nature that imitates art, not vice versa. The meaning of this is that we have been conditioned by our upbringing, by our cultural influences, to see reality in a certain way. If, for instance, someone has been addicted to the reading of comic strips, he may see the people he comes into contact with in the frame of reference of his favorite comic-strip characters. Dostoyevsky gives us the unwelcome truth behind convention.

Gide distinguishes several strata in Dostoyevsky's characters: that of the intelligence, of the passions, and of heavenly illumination. The third is a sacred area from which the intellect is banished and where the passions cannot penetrate. The intelligence is the perfidious, demonic realm, the element of the underground man. Hell, to Dostoyevsky, is the region of the intellect; he depreciates it in a fashion one might call evangelical. It is opposed to the kingdom of God where only those who have renounced their individuality can enter. The intelligence is also morbid, because it freezes action in us. The active man is mediocre. He is governed by his passions but he lacks understanding, and does not have to face the torments, the dilemmas of the intellectual which always result in passiveness.

Gide finds a remarkable affinity between Dostoyevsky's thought and the tone of William Blake's *The Marriage of Heaven and Hell*. Blake states that desire, when not followed by action, engenders havoc. This, Gide rightly points out, is similar to the underground man's philosophy. But then Gide proceeds to misquote Dostoyevsky in an indefensible manner, asserting that according to Dostoyevsky the man of action of the nineteenth century is a characterless creature. In fact, Dostoyevsky says that it is the man of acute consciousness who lacks character. If this was not a slip on Gide's part, it shows his incomprehension of what Dostoyevsky called character.

Another mistake Gide makes concerns the use of monologue. He mentions that Valery Larbaud recently stated that James Joyce, the author of *Ulysses,* was the inventor of this type of narrative. But, Gide contends, Dostoyevsky's *Notes from Underground* is written as a monologue and even carries to perfection all the possibilities contained in such a literary form. Gide does not realize that Joyce's technique is substantially different: first of all, it is not merely the internal monologue, but the stream of consciousness, compounded of sense perceptions, emotive experience, and cognition. Joyce tries to suggest these as they happen to the subject. Dostoyevsky follows an age-old method, that of the fictitious diary. The underground man simply writes down what he thinks. Dostoyevsky does not try to transport us directly into his head, as he would have to if he employed the stream-of consciousness technique. On the other hand, it is true that at certain times his descriptions approach the directness, the ellipses of the thinking process. Essentially, though, *Notes from Underground* is not a stream-of-consciousness, nor even an internal-monologue novel. It is a psychological novel containing perceptions of the highest sensitivity and acuity. It does so by description and analysis, not direct transcription of experience. The difference is of form, of technique, not of content or substance.

In the period between the two world wars, Dostoyevsky's stature rose to ever greater heights, for reasons that we have been stressing up to now: his psychological insight, his concept of personality, his exploration of uncharted areas of the soul. The Russian religious philosopher Dmitri Merezhkovsky, in a study published in 1899, still found fault with the lack of harmony and symmetry in Dostoyevsky's work. The French essayist Andre Suares in his *Trois hommes: Pascal, Ibsen, Dostoievski* (1913) already saw the Russian writer as great just because of the internal conflict existing in him, though he believed that Dostoyevsky transcended all contradictions on the religious plane. Paul Claudel, the celebrated Catholic poet and dramatist, came even closer to the modern perspective on Dostoyevsky when he stated that the Russian was "the inventor of the polymorph character." That is, the great classics have characters that are all of one piece. Dostoyevsky made a psychological discovery that Claudel claims is the equivalent of De Vries' biological discovery of spontaneous mutation. A character all of a sudden undergoes a mutation: features appear in him that beforehand were not there at all. It is this unforeseeable, unknown factor in human nature that is Dostoyevsky's great contribution.

GASSET

The Spanish philosopher Ortega Y Gasset gives an outstanding place to Dostoyevsky in his brilliant study, *Ideas sobra la novela (Considerations On the Novel),* published in 1925. Ortega's thesis is that in the development of the modern novel the part of the plot diminishes, while the importance of the psychology, the analysis of temperament increases. This puts *Notes from Underground* very high on the list of modernity, for it has no plot to speak of. Most of the *Notes* consists of character analysis. Stefan Zweig, the eminent Austrian author, wrote that Dostoyevsky's discoveries had become part and parcel of our culture. Dostoyevsky has been accepted, the truth he has shown us has ceased to be controversial.

MANN

In 1945 the world-renowned German writer Thomas Mann wrote a preface for a new American edition of Dostoyevsky's short novels. He states that Dostoyevsky was among his deepest youthful experiences. Mann discusses especially those aspects of Dostoyevsky's art that are related to his own favorite themes. He sees in Dostoyevsky the diseased genius, the "pale criminal," the Byzantine Christian. His illness, epilepsy, is characterized by an incomparable sense of rapture and ecstasy preceding the spasms. The spasm itself begins with an inarticulate scream and is followed by depression and grief, a sense of spiritual ruin, desolation, and guilt. Mann is of the opinion that Dostoyevsky's epilepsy was a transference of sex dynamics into the realm of the mystical. Disease stimulates the growth of genius - of course, a great deal depends on just who is sick. Perhaps all geniuses are ill, but all who are ill certainly are not geniuses. In cases like Nietzche's and Dostoyevsky's, disease bore fruits that have become more beneficial to life, to humanity, than any healthy normality. Civilization cannot subsist on health alone. The great invalids are Christ figures who take upon themselves the ills, the sufferings, the sins of the world. Dostoyevsky was such a figure, as is his creation, the underground man. The average man's healthfulness feeds upon the disease of the genius. But health and disease are, in any case, tricky terms. The real test is not superficial harmony and soundness of body, but how much morbidity an individual can absorb and yet survive. Dostoyevsky's illness was not a privation, a minus, but a product of superabundant power, an excess of health.

Mann considers *Notes from Underground* to be the most significant of the author's short novels. He admits that he likes Part I even better than the second part. Its denial of progress, humanitarianism, and meliorism may sound like sacrilege, an invitation to chaos and destruction, but it is actually truth, the dark side of truth, which we cannot suppress, even if we would like to. This is the gist of Mann's article. Though Mann does not state this explicitly in his Dostoyevsky study, the most important agreement between his and the underground man's views is that both regard intelligence as a disease, though their terminology is different. What the underground man calls acute consciousness is the same, or practically the same, as the spirit in Thomas Mann's lexicon. The conviction that the spirit is an anti-vital force was an obsessive preoccupation with Mann, especially in his early period. But in the present article he apparently wanted to emphasize the healing, restorative power of genius.

The existentialist movement, which suddenly began to enjoy unprecedented popularity after World War II, greeted the tortured anti-hero of the underground as a blood brother of the anguished twentieth-century intellectual. Though Sartre himself never devoted an entire study to Dostoyevsky, affinities between the underground man and some of the French existentialist's protagonists: Roquentin (see No. 5 in the section Essay Questions and Answers), the narrator in the story Erostrate, Daniel in *Les Chemins de la liberte* (*Roads to Freedom*), are so striking as to suggest a deep personal influence. As William Phillips rightly observes, the new human type of the underground man, which is Dostoyevsky's creation in literature, is immediately recognizable as the tragic man of sensibility of modern writing. Robert Jackson in his Dostoyevsky's *Underground Man in Russian Literature* subscribes to the consensus regarding the relevance of the book for our times, asserting that the **catastrophe** of two world wars, the nightmare of concentration camps, and the threat of atomic annihilation have shaken our belief in a rational world. The collapse of a universe guided by reason created the protean type of the modern existentialist hero, a direct descendant of the underground man.

NOTES FROM THE UNDERGROUND

ESSAY QUESTIONS AND ANSWERS

....

Question: Does the title of Part 2, *Apropos of the Wet Snow,* convey any symbolic meaning?

Answer: Though the underground man says that he gave this heading to the second part of the *Notes* because it was on a sleety day that he started writing it, the title is not merely the product of a moment's whim but is indicative of thematic structure. This is not exactly what we call pathetic fallacy in literature (the ascribing of human characteristics to natural phenomena), but rather a chance correspondence between the weather and the underground man's permanent spiritual condition which is exploited for purposes of symbolism. Estranged from human intercourse, he vegetates in a spiritual underworld that is musty, moldy, and fetid. His apartment, his hole where he buries himself, is also a physical correlative of his mental state. There is an interesting parallel, too, between the narrator's psychological condition and his depicting of the future that awaits Liza. He is living in a spiritual hell. In order to frighten her away from her present occupation, he wants to describe hell to her, and to do so he instinctively resorts to imagery expressive of his state. They will throw her into a putrid cellar when she gets old. They will bury her on a sleety day, and there will be melted snow in her grave. The hell that his overdeveloped intellectuality caused in him is parallel with the physical degradation of a social outcast, a prostitute.

Question: What, if any, is the social message of the *Notes*?

Answer: The book reflects total disillusionment with melioristic social philosophies. It denies that man will ever be guided by his enlightened self-interest. It claims that, human nature being what it is, nothing can permanently solve the problems we confront. We want the unattainable, and even if we reach the goals we are now setting for ourselves we shall be no better off. Once attained, these goals become meaningless. Western thinkers are dreamers, and their dreams can never be translated into reality.

Yet curiously there is another aspect to the *Notes*. Dostoyevsky is on both sides of the fence. On the one hand, he no longer believes in social progress, at least not in what was then the Western sense. On the other hand, the old rebel still cries out in him at certain times. This is evident in his school reminiscences, in the way he speaks of his colleagues when an assessor, in the incident with the haughty officer, and in his description of the fate of old prostitutes. He cries out against social injustice, but thinks there is no remedy for it. The only real values are to be found in people who are in close contact with the soil. It is not easy to see, though, how the conditions existing in Russia in the nineteenth century would have been helped by the pochvennik's doctrine. If the intellectuals were as rotten, evil, and phantasmal as Dostoyevsky suggests, how could they have possibly helped the peasantry? Perhaps it would have helped them to strike new roots in the ethnic soil, but their influence would have been harmful. They did not even have anything practical to impart to the peasantry, according to Dostoyevsky, who considered technical progress itself as pernicious.

Question: Who have been some of the underground man's descendants in modern literature?

Answer: The typical modern protagonist is an anti-hero. As such, the list would be too long to give here. But narrowing the context to the underground man's difficulty in defining himself, his introspective tendencies, his incapacity to act, and his alienation, we can still produce an impressive catalogue of important works.

The Swedish dramatist August Strindberg (1849-1912) insisted in his preface to the play *Miss Julie* that the modern character is disjointed. In earlier ages, he said, the word character used to denote a man who had become fixed in his nature or who had perfectly adapted himself to a particular role in life, whereas those who "sailed not with sheets set fast, but who veered down the wind to stay closer to the wind again" were considered to be lacking in character. In our changing times, he said, flexibility has become the ideal; only those elastic enough can survive. Thus, the modern barometer of character is the capacity to change, to adapt oneself to varying circumstances.

The Italian novelist Italo Svevo (1861-1928) in *La coscienza di Zeno* (*Zeno*) describes a weak-willed, hypochondriac man who, because of his analytical mind, cannot reach any decisions. Zeno's particular difficulty is to fashion a personality for himself.

Sicilian-born Luigi Pirandello (1867-1936) staked his whole artistic career on tackling the enigmas of personality, the roles and masks we assume in social life, and the relationship between our true self and the image we have of ourselves. He wrote many plays, some of the most remarkable being: *Enrico IV (Henry IV),* the story of a man who goes insane because it is only in madness that role and being became identical in him; *Questa sera si recita a soggetto* (*Tonight We Improvise*), in which conventional and theatrical roles are interchanged to the point of confusing the audience; and *Come tu mi vuoi* (*As You Want Me*), where he shows how one modifies one's character in order to suit the image others form of us. His best-known novel, *Il fu Mattia Pascal* (*The Late Mathias Pascal*) recounts the story of a man who throws away his "official" police-file personality to become someone else.

Andre Gide (1869-1951), whose artistic program was sincerity at any cost, strove to expose the falsehoods contained in the artificial front we put up before the external world. *Le Promethee mal enchaine' (Prometheus Ill-Bound)* probes the mystery of freedom. *Les Faux-Monnayeurs (The Counter-feiters)*, his only novel, is a study of character along Dostoyevskian lines.

Thomas Mann (1875-1955) in his monumental Joseph tetralogy sheds light on the dynamism of mythical identification. He illustrates how the myth provides a frame of reference in which we feel more secure and which lends meaning and pattern to a chaotic world. He indicates that the major human roles can be traced back to an almost endless series of historical archetypes.

Robert Musil (1880-1942) in his cycle of novels *Der Mann ohne Eigenschaften* (*The Man Without Qualities*) examines the consciousness of Ulrich, in whom intelligence has replaced instinct and emotion. He lacks qualities in much the same way the underground man does. As ideas are possible realities, he prefers to play with his potentialities in his imagination rather than apply them in crude actuality.

Franz Kafka (1883-1924) explores the irrational in the world rather than in the subject. His **protagonist**, K., is the underground man's cousin in his alienation, guilt feeling, and inability to cope with the demands of his environment. In *Der Prozess* (*The Trial*) he is arrested and tortured without any reason. He protests against the injustice, yet inwardly he feels he is culpable. In *Das Schloss* (*The Castle*) K. tries to get recognition from the unknown authorities who are running the affairs of this world according to a logic inscrutable to ordinary intelligence.

Albert Camus (1913-1960) similarly started out from his perception of the irrational. His heroes are the great rebels who opposed the wanton cruelty, senseless suffering, and meaningless existence in the universe. His most popular work, *L'Etranger* (*The Stranger*), illustrates the absurdity of the human condition; his last novel, *La Chute* (*The Fall*) despairs of the possibility of sincerely selfless action beyond the gestures and roles of meretricious social interplay.

Jean-Paul Sartre (1905-) bases his philosophical system on the premise of man's undefinability. Consciousness, he believes, is the introduction of nothingness into the world. It is a kind of mirror that reflects reality but is nothing by itself. Hence man is condemned to a permanent lack of identity; in Sartre's terms, "he is not what he is." All his efforts to capture himself as an in-itself, that is, an essence that can exist independently, not just as a function, must be unavailing. The Sartrean character most closely resembling the underground man is Roquentin in *La Nausee* (*Nausea*). Also consult Question 5.

Question: Did Dostoyevsky's negative view of intelligence have its sole support in romantic anti-intellectualism?

Answer: Dostoyevsky's German romantic predecessors provided only the immediate influence. There is usually more than a superficial or coincidental reason for an author's adherence to a doctrine as basic as this. The real reason must be searched for in his temperament, upbringing, or childhood environment. Anti-intellectualism is probably as old as mankind. The Bible, which is among our most venerable records, ascribes the fall of man to his curiosity, to his having eaten of the fruit of the tree of knowledge. Thus wisdom has been represented as having a curse on it since our earliest recorded history. Even in Greek mythology, Prometheus, who stole fire from heaven for the benefit of man, thereby starting the development of technical progress, was punished by Zeus. In this case too, knowledge was regarded as evil - a good for man, but an evil in the absolute sense, for God is the supreme arbiter over good and bad.

This view, therefore, has its place among our most pious traditions. Dostoyevsky's father, physician in a state-owned hospital and therefore a civil servant, belonged to a segment of Russian society which did not revere intellect or originality. Despite his early revolt, which ended in conviction and hard labor in Siberia, Dostoyevsky by his middle years seems to have adopted most of the standards imposed on him as a child. The conviction that a more than average portion of brains is detrimental may very well have been among these standards.

Question: Compare the underground man with Meursault in Camus' *The Stranger* and with Roquentin in Sartre's *Nausea.*

Answer: Meursault is even less of a rebel than the underground man. He accepts things as they are with fatalistic imperturbability; he does not complain about anything, including his capital punishment. Meursault is no thinker, and the entire question of overconsciousness and identity is devoid of interest to him. He resembles the underground man in his alienation, though most of the time Meursault has no real awareness of his estrangement. Why and in what manner is he alienated? His problem is simply that he is absolutely sincere, to himself as well as others, and this sets him apart and evokes the incredulous horror of society. Thus, the most important connection between Meursault and the underground man is sincerity - with the latter, sincerity is the product of conscious striving, with the former, it is taken for granted, being an unquestioned attitude toward the world.

With Roquentin, the relationship is closer. First, the question of freedom is crucial to both. Antoine Roquentin senses that he is free and tries to hide his freedom from himself so as not to be forced to act. He assumes as a substitute personality and a vicarious means of living, the Marquis de Rollebon. The underground man, on the other hand, tries to prove to himself more or less successfully that his will is free.

They are equally frustrated, and equally hate the routine of their lives. The underground man periodically withdraws to his dream world, while Roquentin takes refuge in his studies of the Marquis's times. Roquentin discovers that adventures exist only in books; man is contingent (unnecessary), and the intuitive grasp of man's condition causes his nausea. The underground man, too, is after experiences such as are described in books and is forced to admit that they cannot be realized. At the very core of the predicament of both is their lack of self-identity, their nothingness. What is so remarkable about the **protagonist** of the *Notes* is that he precedes his French existentialist counterpart by over eighty years, already containing most of the important elements that have made Sartre's fame and fortune in contemporary literature.

Question: Dostoyevsky was first captivated by Jeremy Bentham's utilitarianism and by the doctrines of the French utopian socialists Proudhon and Fourier. The *Notes* express disenchantment with these philosophies. Outline the principles of utilitarianism and utopian socialism as propounded by Bentham (1748-1832), Fourier (1772-1837), and Proudhon (1809-1865).

Answer: Bentham's only test of value was usefulness. He believed that all of man's actions were guided by two considerations: search for pleasure and avoidance of pain. We may pretend that we are not subject to this law, but in reality we cannot abjure it. He said that his principle of utility recognized this subjection and made it the foundation of the entire system, which was based on the attainment of maximum pleasure with the aid of reason and lawful order. The "community" as such is an abstraction; the aim of good government is to secure the well-being of the largest possible number of individuals.

Bentham worked out a list of pleasures and pains, with subdivisions. For instance, under sensual pleasures he subsumed taste, hearing, seeing, smelling, touch, etc. He set up what he called a felicilic calculus, measuring the duration, intensity, and closeness of each of these sensations. By means of this he hoped to lend the exactness of natural science to his system. While he was not in favor of an omnipotent state apparatus, he speculated that government should step in to amend the situation whenever the good of the greater number was in jeopardy.

Fourier based his doctrine on the scale of passions. People, he argued, are drawn to each other and to things by the force of different passions, which he proceeded to catalogue. Society as he knew it frustrated these passions. He proposed therefore to create model units, called phalanxes, to put his system to a test. In each phalanx there would be capitalists, managers, and workers. Profit would be divided among them, with the workers getting the largest share. He recommended a rugged schedule of about fourteen hours' labor a day for workers, but he said this would be amply compensated for by an appeal to their sense of variety: they would not work for over two hours on any one task. Those performing the more difficult or less desirable chores would be paid more. All the members of each phalanx would live together in a kind of hotel, eating in the common dining room. He had various schemes for lessening the monotony of routine jobs. He sat in his office at certain specified hours for over a decade waiting for an enterprising capitalist to show up. Though no one actually offered to give his ideas a try during his lifetime, Fourier exercised a considerable influence on intellectuals in Russia and elsewhere.

Proudhon was publishing his works at the time Dostoyevsky was in his twenties. His social reforms were not based on communal living. He was an individualist. His conception was that free credit should be given to every citizen. He deplored the lending of money on interest. He wanted to replace the class of capitalists with state-supported financing of deserving private businesses and other undertakings. He asserted that property was theft, though he later specified that by property he only meant income gained from capital investment. His theory of mutualism envisaged the establishment of cooperatives through associations of producers, such as now operate in a number of countries.

NOTES FROM THE UNDERGROUND

BIBLIOGRAPHY

WORKS BY FYODOR DOSTOYEVSKY

We have listed the titles in English translation. The publishing houses named are those whose editions of the respective works are currently available to the student in this country. The dates, given in parentheses, always refer to the publication dates in the original Russian, thereby providing a convenient source of reference.

The Brothers Karamazov. Modern Library. (1880)

Crime and Punishment. Bantam. (1866)

The Diary of a Writer. Braziller. (1873-1881)

A Disgraceful Affair. Dufour. (1862)

The Double. Indiana. (1846)

The Eternal Husband, and Other Stories. Macmillan. (1870)

The Friend of the Family. Holt, Rinehart, and Winston. (1859)

The Honest Thief. Macmillan. (1848)

The House of the Dead. Dell. (1861)

The Idiot. Bantam. (1868)

The Insulted and Injured. Grove. (1861)

Letters. (Dostoyevsky's correspondence.) McGraw.

Netochka Nezvanova. Van Nostrand. (1849)

Notes from Underground. Laurel. (1864)

Poor Folk (1864) and *The Gambler.* Dutton. (1867)

The Possessed. Modern Library. (1872)

A Raw Youth. Dell. (1875)

Short Novels. In addition to those listed in this bibliography, this volume includes *Uncle's Dream* (1859). Dial.

Short Stories. In addition to those listed in this bibliography, the volume includes the following stories: "Mr. Prohartchin" (1846), "A Novel in Nine Letters" (1847), "The Landlady" (1847), "Polzunkov" (1848), "A Faint Heart" (1848), "Another Man's Wife or the Husband Under the Bed" (1848), "A Christmas Tree and a Wedding" (1848), "White Nights" (1848), "A Little Hero" (1857), "An Unpleasant Predicament" (1862), "The Crocodile" (1865), "Bobok" (1873), "The Peasant Marey" (1876), "The Heavenly Christmas Tree" (1876), "A Gentle Spirit" (1876), "The Dream of a Ridiculous Man" (1877). Dial.

WORKS ON DOSTOYEVSKY

For an exhaustive bibliography, the student is referred to Vladimir Seduro's *Dostoyevsky in Russian Literary Criticism 1846-1956,* New York, 1957.

Abraham, Gerald E. H., *Dostoevsky.* London, 1936. A short, general introduction. Not particularly challenging.

Carr, Edward H., *Dostoevsky. A new biography.* London, 1931. Revised edition, 1949.

Coulson, Jessie., *Dostoyevsky. A Self-Portrait.* London, 1962. Based on the Russian author's autobiographical revelations.

Hingley, Ronald, *The Undiscovered Dostoyevsky.* New York, 1962. An interesting study, modern in approach.

Lauth, Reinhard, "Ich habe die Wahrheit gesehen." *Die Philosophie Dostojewskijs.* The best German work of contemporary scholarship, a systematic **exposition** of Dostoyevsky's thought. Not available in English.

Lavrin, Janko, *Dostoevsky and His Creation. A Psycho-Critical Study.* The author is a distinguished Dostoevsky scholar. Comprehensive, perceptive, and clearly stated.

Lloyd, John A. T., *Fyodor Dostoevsky.* New York, 1947. This is a new edition of a somewhat antiquated work.

Lukacs, Georg, "Dostojewskij," *Der russische Realismus in der Weltliteratur.* Berlin, 1949. Lukacs is a Marxist esthete, of his school the most widely recognized in the West. Has not been translated into English.

Madaule, Jacques, *Dostoievski.* Paris, 1956. Gives modern French perspective on Dostoyevsky in concise form.

Magarshak, David, *Dostoevsky.* New York, 1962. An exhaustive critical study.

Muchnic, Helen, *Dostoevsky's English Reputation.* Northampton, 1939. Useful guide on the subject, but does not include anything after 1936.

Murry, John Middleton, *Fyodor Dostoevsky. A Critical Study.* New York, 1916. Murry was a distinguished English critic. Some of his observations are still pertinent.

Passage, Charles E., *Dostoevski the Adapter. A Study in Dostoevski's Use of the Tales of Hoffmann.* Chapel Hill, 1954. Sheds light on the influence of German romanticism on Dostoyevsky.

Payne, Pierre S. R., *Dostoyevsky. A Human Portrait.* New York, 1961. Emphasizes the biographical aspect.

Simmons, Ernest J., *Dostoevsky. The Making of a Novelist.* New York, 1940. *New edition*, 1950. Has valuable bibliography. Simmons is a well-known critic who has reviewed the 19th-century and contemporary Russian literary scene from various points of view.

Soloviev, Evgenii, *Dostoievsky. His Life and Literary Activity.* A Biographical Sketch. New York, 1916.

Stammler, Heinrich, "Dostoevsky's Aesthetics and Schelling's Philosophy of Art," *Comparative Literature* 7, 1955. The influence of German romantic idealism on Dostoyevsky.

Suares, Andre, *Trois Hommes: Pascal, Ibsen, Dostoievski.* Paris, 1913. NRF edition, 1935. Suares was an essayist and religious thinker who played an important part in the movement for spiritual revival after the turn of the century. His Dostoyevsky study is highly personal and lyrical, not a work of scholarship but an important milestone in the Russian's Western reputation. Untranslated.

Troyat, Henri, Firebrand. *The Life of Dostoevsky*. London, 1946. English translation of work by French academician, novelist, critic, and playwright, born in Russia. He regards Dostoyevsky as his greatest master and is one of his most popular present-day interpreters.

Woodhouse, Cristopher M., *Dostoievsky*. London, 1951. A short introduction for the general reader.

Yarmolinsky, Avrahm, *Dostoevsky. His Life and Art*. New York, 1957. Expanded edition of a study originally published in 1934. The author is a specialist on modern Russian literature. The work is mainly biographical.

ON NOTES FROM UNDERGROUND

Bercovitch, Sacvan, "Dramatic **Irony** in *Notes from the Underground*," *Slavic and East European Journal*, VIII, 1964. Helpful discussion of a significant aspect of the *Notes*. The student interested in further research along the same lines is advised to consult Morton Gurewitch's *European Romantic Irony* (New York, 1957), H. W. Hewett-Thayer's *Hoffmann, Author of the Tales* (Princeton, 1948), Laura Hofrichter's *Heinrich Heine* (Oxford, 1963), and Jean-Paul Sartre's *Baudelaire* (trans.: Norfolk, 1950).

Berdyaev, Nicholas, *Dostoevsky. First American edition*, New York, 1934. Published by *Meridian Books*, 1957. This book on Dostoyevsky's philosophy and psychology as well as his religious struggle was among the first to recognize the importance of the *Notes*. See also the section titled Critical Commentary.

Carrier, Warren, "Artistic Form and Unity in *Notes from the Underground*," *Renascence*, XV, 1964. On this issue, see Question 1 in the Essay Questions and Answers section.

Gide, Andre, *Dostoievski*. Paris, 1923. French available in paperback, in the popular NRF Idees series. The latest American edition is by *New Directions* (1949). Generally recognized as one of the most original and probing analyses on Dostoyevsky. Regards the *Notes* as the key to the Russian author's production. Not a work of meticulous scholarship, it is an example of creative criticism. While Gide was composing his Dostoyevsky study he was also at work on his chef d'oeuvre, *Les Faux-Monnayeurs (The Counterfeiters,* New York, 1927), which is recommended as collateral reading. See Critical Commentary section.

Jackson, Robert L., *Dostoevsky's Underground Man in Russian Literature*. '*S-Gravenhage*, 1958. Indispensable to the study of the *Notes* not only because it lists and reviews some important source materials but also as a perceptive critical contribution on its own. Jackson's main thesis is that the underground man "symbolizes the divorce of the Russian Europeanized educated class from the life of the people." He recognizes in the underground man the prototype of the modern existentialist hero. He stresses the disintegration of consciousness. From an academic point of view, the fault of Jackson's study is that terms like reason, dynamic, etc. are used too loosely.

Mann, Thomas, *Dostoevsky - in Moderation.* This study, published in German by *Neue Rundschau*, 1945-46, under the title Dostojewski - mit Massen, serves as an introduction to the *Short Novels of Dostoevsky*, Dial, New York, 1945. Cf. the section Critical Commentary, on Mann's appraisal of the *Notes.* See also Zerner, below.

Matlaw, Ralph E., "Structure and Integration in *Notes from the Underground*," Publications of the Modern Language Association, 73, 1958. See Carrier, above.

Phillips, William, "Dostoevsky's Underground Man," *The Short Stories of Dostoevsky*. Dial, New York, 1946. Phillips' theory is that Dostoyevsky was throughout his life motivated by a constant search for authority. While his unconscious had destroyed the father, he had to find a surrogate father image, whether in the Czar, morality, or God. This, according to the author, is the source of the feeling of absurdity, paranoia, guilt, and inadequacy of the underground man, whom Phillips considers as a self-portrait of the Russian master.

Terras, Victor, "Problems of Human Existence in the Works of the Young Dostoevsky," *Slavic Review,* XXIII, 1964. Terras stresses the existentialist aspect. See the Critical Commentary and No. 5 in the Essay Questions and Answers, as well as the background materials given below.

Zerner, Marianne, "Thomas Mann's 'Der Bajazzo', a **parody** of Dostoevsky's *Notes from Underground*," Monatshefte, LVI, 1964. "Der Bajazzo" is one of Mann's early stories, the confessions of a man who feels he is ridiculous in all the circumstances of his life. It is perhaps an exaggeration to say that it is a **parody** of the *Notes.* An interesting topic for a research paper would be the common source of **irony** in Mann and Dostoyevsky, their treatment of intelligence as a disease, their views on alienation, and their concepts of the artistic temperament, taking the similarities between "Der Bajazzo" and the *Notes* as the point of departure. See Mann also in the Critical Commentary and in Number 3 of the Essay Questions and Answers.

BACKGROUND MATERIAL FOR THE NOTES

Following is a list of reading suggestions on various problems raised in *Notes from Underground*.

THE ROMANTIC IDEOLOGY

Brandes, George, *Main Currents in Nineteenth-Century Literature.* 6 vols. New York, 1901-5.

Babbitt, Irving, *Rousseau and Romanticism.* New York, 1919.

Boas, George, *French Philosophies of the Romantic Period.* Baltimore, 1934.

Francke, Kuno, *A History of German Literature as Determined by Social Forces.* New York, 1931.

Brinton, Charles, *Political Ideas of the English Romanticists.* Oxford, 1926.

UTILITARIANISM, UTOPIAN SOCIALISM, POSITIVISM, AND THE TRIUMPH OF SCIENCE

Atkinson, John, *Bentham*, London, 1905.

Bourgin, Henri, *Fourier.* Paris, 1905.

Mill, John Stuart, *Auguste Comte and Positivism.* London, 1965.

Williams, Henry S., *The Story of Nineteenth-Century Science.* New York, 1900.

Dampier-Whetham, John D., *History of Science and Its Relations With Philosophy.* New York, 1932.

LITERARY REALISM AND NATURALISM

Delattre, Genevieve, *Les opinions litteraires de Balzac.* Paris, 1961.

Ferrere, Jean, *L'Esthetique de Gustave Flaubert.* Paris, 1913.

Zola, Emile, *Le Roman experimental.* Paris, 1880.

REACTION AGAINST SCIENCE; IRRATIONALISM

Bergson, Henri, *L'evolution creatrice*. Paris, 1913. Trans.: *Creative Evolution*.

Camus, Albert, *Le Mythe de Sisyphe*. Paris, 1942. Trans.: *The Myth of Sisyphus*, New York, 1955.

Croce, Benedetto, Thomas Mann, A. N. Whitehead, and others, *Freedom, Its Meaning*. New York, 1940.

Malinowski, Bronislaw, *Freedom and Civilization*. New York, 1944.

Peirce, Charles S. *Chance, Love, and Logic.* New York, 1923.

Shotwell, John J., *Freedom, Its History and Meaning*. New York, 1939.

Bendix, Reinhard, *Social Science and the Distrust of Reason*. Berkeley, 1951.

Kaufmann, Walter, ed., *Existentialism from Dostoevsky to Sartre*. New York, 1956.

DEPERSONALIZATION, LOSS OF IDENTITY, DISINTEGRATION OF PERSONALITY

Alberes, R.-M., *L'Adventure intellectuelle du XXe siecle*. Paris, 1959.

Untranslated. Baerwald, Friedrich, "A Sociological View of Depersonalization," *Thought*, XXXI, Spring 1956.

Glicksberg, Charles I., *The Self in Modern Literature*. University Park, Pennsylvania, 1963.

Lynd, Helen Merrell, *On Shame and the Search for Identity*. New York, 1958.

Ortega Y Gasset, Jose, *Man and People.* New York, 1957.

Sartre, Jean-Paul, *L'etre et le neant.* Paris, 1943. Trans.: *Being and Nothingness*, New York, 1953.

ALIENATION

Arendt, Hannah, *The Human Condition.* Chicago, 1958.

Lowith, Karl, "Man's Self-Alienation in the Early Writings of Marx," *Social Research*, XXI, Summer 1954.

Pappenheim, Fritz, *The Alienation of Modern Man.* New York, 1959.

Wilson, Colin, *The Outsider.* London, 1957. *

CHRONOLOGICAL TABLE

We have arranged in tabular form the important events in the life of Dostoyevsky. For publication dates of his works, see the Bibliography.

1821 October 30, born in Moscow, the son of Dr. Dostoyevsky and his wife, Maria, nee Nechayeva.

1834 Dr. Dostoyevsky purchases an estate in Darovoye.

1837 Fyodor's mother dies.

1838 Fyodor is sent to Saint Petersburg to attend engineering school.

1839 His father is murdered by his serfs.

1841 He graduates from engineering school.

1843 He takes a position in the War Ministry.

1844 Dostoyevsky quits his job. He decides to live by his pen.

1844-1845 He does translations.

1846 He is launched on his literary career through his friendship with Nekrassov. First successes.

1846-1849 Dostoyevsky becomes a member and collaborates in the work of Petrashevsky's revolutionary group.

1849 He is arrested, tried, and condemned to die. His sentence is commuted to four years' hard labor in Siberia.

1850-1854 Imprisonment in the penal colony of Omsk.

1854-1859 Serves in the Russian Army at Semipalatinsk, Siberia.

1857 He marries Maria Dmitriyevna Isayeva and adopts her son Pasha.

1859 Dostoyevsky is permitted to return to European Russia. He goes to Tver and then to Saint Petersburg.

1860 He founds the periodical Vremia.

1861-1865 Friendship with Polina Suslova.

1862 First trip to Europe. He visits Germany, France, England, Switzerland, Italy, and Austria.

1863 Second European trip, with Polina. Gambling losses at Wiesbaden.

1864 Dostoyevsky's wife and his brother Michael die.

1865 New sojourn in Western Europe. Wiesbaden, Copenhagen. Break with Polina.

1867 Second marriage with Anna Grigorievna.

1867-1871 The Dostoyevskys live in Western Europe, first in Germany and Switzerland. Heavy gambling losses.

1868 They move to Italy. Their first daughter is born, but dies two months later.

1869 They move back to Germany. Birth of their second daughter.

1871 Birth of their first son, Fyodor.

1873 The Dostoyevskys rent a house at Staraya Russa, by Lake Ilmen.

1875 Last, short sojourn in Western Europe. Birth of their second son, Alyosha, who dies three years later.

1878 Dostoyevsky becomes a member of the Russian Academy.

1880 Speech at Pushkin festival in Moscow.

1881 January 28, Dostoyevsky dies after an internal hemorrhage.

www.ingramcontent.com/pod-product-compliance
Lightning Source LLC
LaVergne TN
LVHW011732060526
838200LV00051B/3149